knead

knead

expert breads• baguettes• pretzels• brioche• pastries• pizza• pastas• pies

carol tennant

LAUREL GLEN

San Diego, California

Published in the United States by
Laurel Glen Publishing
An imprint of the Advantage Publishers Group
5880 Oberlin Drive, San Diego, CA 92121-4794
www.advantagebooksonline.com

Copyright © MQ Publications Limited 2001
Text © Carol Tennant 2001
Project Editor: Kate John
Designer: Elizabeth Ayer
Photography: Janine Hosegood
Stylist: Vanessa Kellas

All notations of errors or omissions should be addressed to Laurel Glen Publishing, editorial department, at the above address. All other correspondence (author inquiries, permissions and rights) concerning the content of this book should be addressed to MQ Publications, 12 The Ivories, 6–8 Northampton Street, London, England N1 2HY.

ISBN 1-57145-585-X
Library of Congress Cataloging-in-Publication Data available on request.

1 2 3 4 04 03 02 01

Printed and bound in England by Butler & Tanner Ltd

contents

introduction

Making your own bread conjures up a cozy kitchen—and that glorious, unforgettable smell as it bakes. Bread is a lot easier to make in your own kitchen than you might think, as are pasta and pastry. Flour is the ingredient common to all three baking methods, and you'll need to know a little about the difference between them before you start. Gluten is the vital ingredient in wheat flour that gives bread its "spring," holds pasta together, and gives pastry its flaky texture.

texture **White bread flour:** all the recipes calling for this have been tested using a high-quality unbleached flour. In the United States, a good source of unbleached bread flour is probably a natural food shop or specialty mail order supplier, while in Europe it is more widely available. The recipes will work with bleached flour of course, but the flavor will not be as good. Bread flour has a high gluten content, typically between 11.5% and 14%. Aside from bleaching, steel-grinding, the most common method of wheat grinding, also affects the gluten levels in the resulting flour. Heat from friction is generated during this type of fast grinding and this tends to damage the gluten level as well as the various vitamins and enzymes found naturally in the wheat germ. These often have to be added back into the ground flour. Stonegrinding—a slower process producing far less heat and a better flour—is becoming more common and it is worth seeking out suppliers of stoneground flour.

All-purpose flour: this is the type of flour most commonly used in other types of baking and is also known as "soft" flour. The gluten content is usually between 9% and 11%. Soft flours are mostly used with chemical raising agents in wet batters for making cakes or pastry.

Self-rising or cake flour: all-purpose flour to which baking powder has been added.

00 Italian pasta flour: as a general rule, 00 flour is a hard flour with a high gluten content most commonly used for making pasta. If necessary, white bread flour can be substituted.

kneading When you make bread, the dough is kneaded until the gluten "sets up." Gluten is formed by the combination of two proteins, gliadin, and glutenin, that exist in high quantities in wheat flour. When these protein fragments are hydrated with water, or other liquid, they bond with each other creating a large protein aggregate—the gluten—which gives bread and pasta doughs their structure and strength. The longer the dough is kneaded (between 6–15 minutes is typical), the stronger the gluten becomes and the springier the dough feels. However, the friction of

kneading causes the temperature of the dough to rise. If you work a dough too long and too hard (for instance in a machine) the heat begins to break the gluten apart and the dough will become unusable. This seldom happens when hand kneading. In pastry making, handling the dough should remain light to ensure it stays as cool as possible. Overmixing will make a tough, instead of flaky, dough. If you decide to knead bread dough in a food processor, it is best to do it in bursts of 30–45 seconds and then to allow the dough to cool before continuing, to prevent overheating.

equipment

ceramic baking beans
For baking pastry "blind." The beans help
to ensure an evenly baked pastry case.

nest of biscuit cutters
Fluted style cutters are ideal
for making filled pasta.

brioche pan The steep sides assist
the dough to rise during baking.

**wooden
chopping board**
A sturdy board is best
for slicing bread on:

9-inch fluted tart pan
A loose base makes it easier to
serve a flan whole.

pizza stone
By maintaining an even heat during baking, the
stone is ideal and can be used to serve the pizza.

baking tray
Ideal for baking rolls and round loaves.

2-pound loaf pan
A staple piece of baking equipment.

mixer with dough hook
Useful for maximizing the elasticity of dough,
but care is needed to avoid overheating the dough.

pasta drying rack
A simple, but efficient way to
dry pasta strands evenly.

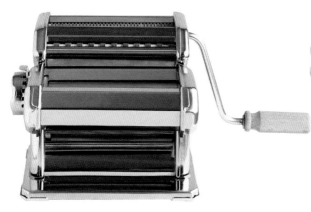

pasta machine
It cuts pasta-making
time in half.

**pasta machine with ravioli
attachment**
A simple way to prepare ravioli.

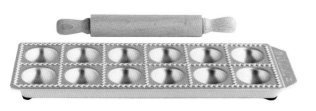

ravioli tray and rolling pin
This kit is a useful alternative to the
pasta machine attachment.

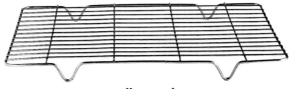

cooling rack
Prevents breads from acquiring a
soggy base during cooling.

bread knife A serrated blade cuts all types of bread.

small paring knife
A useful tool for trimming pastry and pasta.

scalpel
A handy implement for scoring across bread doughs before baking.

wooden spoons
For mixing yeast into flour.

dishtowel
Use to cover dough during rising.

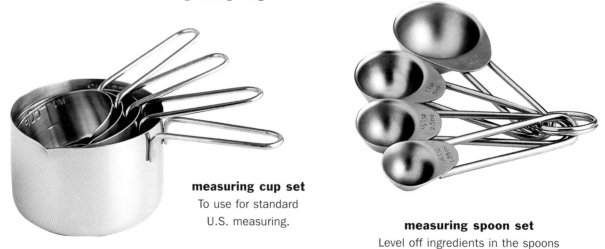

measuring cup set
To use for standard U.S. measuring.

measuring spoon set
Level off ingredients in the spoons for accuracy.

sieve
Stainless steel
is best for
sifting all flours.

measuring cup
Accurate measuring of liquids in
dough making is important.

weighing scale
Careful measuring will reap the
best dough results.

oil mister
For lightly spraying dough
before it rises.

flour sifter
For flouring work surfaces.

zigzag cutter
Ideal for sealing
filled pasta
shapes, and for
creating lattice
pastry tops.

**cheese
grater**
Handy for
grating fresh
Parmesan.

pastry brushes
Flat or round bristle—
used for applying
glaze finishes to
bread and pastry.

**rolling
pin**
Wooden
and
cylindrical
are best for
rolling out
pastry
evenly.

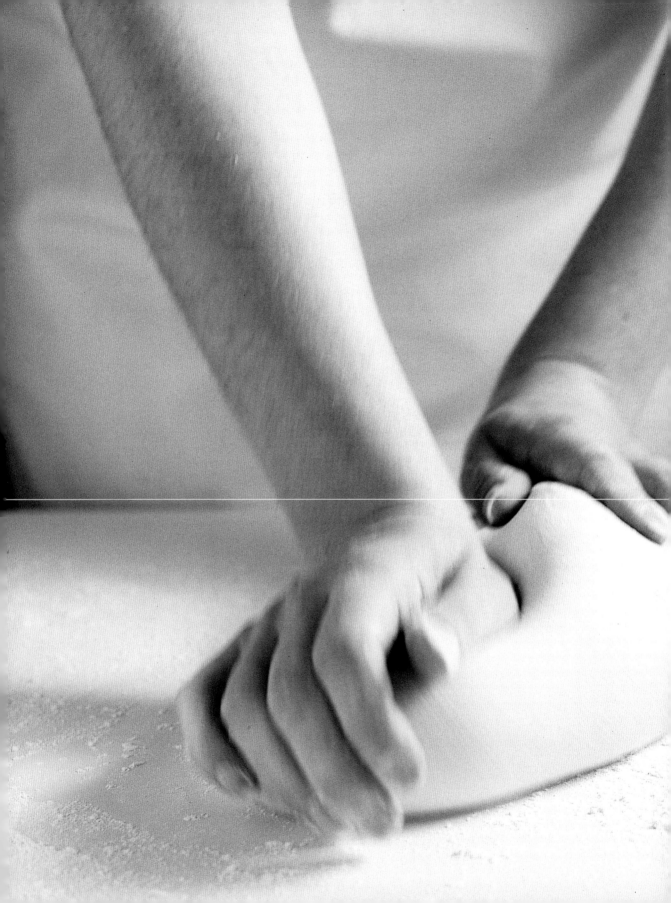

bread

bread introduction Is there anything more tantalizing than the aroma of fresh bread, just out of the oven? Many people believe that bread-making is a long-lost traditional skill, surrounded by myth and mystique. The truth is, it couldn't be easier. Apart from flour, the other main ingredients in a loaf of bread are yeast, water, salt, and some type of sugar. That's it. Yet the number of possible combinations appear to be endless and the different results you can achieve by varying one or the other of these constituents is astonishing. For example, when making bagels the dough is so firm that it can

burn the motor out on a mixer. A dough that is made with little water like bagels (see page 30) produces a bread with a close textured crumb. Other doughs, like ciabatta (see page 36) or spiced potato bread (see page 29) recipes are so wet they can't be kneaded by hand and have a very open texture, almost glossy crumb with lots of large holes. To guide you, each recipe describes whether the dough should be soft, sticky, or firm.

Which yeast? **Fresh yeast:** this is the stuff that gives bread its name for being difficult. Fresh yeast is available from supermarkets, health-food shops, and specialty baking stores, but must be absolutely fresh or it will be unreliable. Commercial yeast is a by-product of the brewing industry. When fresh, it should be creamy colored, moist, and firm, with a strong "yeasty" smell. If it is crumbly or has discolored dark patches, it is probably stale. Fresh yeast comes in a compressed cake form. To use, simply dissolve in the liquid specified in the recipe, along with a little sugar and/or flour, until it is frothy and active before being added to the flour. It only keeps for a few days, wrapped up in the fridge, but will freeze for up to three months in an airtight container or plastic bag.

Dried yeast: this is essentially fresh yeast that has been dried and preserved in packages or jars. Use it in the same way as fresh yeast by dissolving it in the liquid then leaving it to froth before adding it to the flour.

Instant yeast: all the recipes in this book call for this type of dried yeast. It is highly reliable and so easy to use, as it is added directly to the flour. In a few of the recipes the yeast is mixed with some of the other ingredients and left to "sponge" for up to several hours. This lets the yeast become very active, but also allows the flavor of the mixture to develop, giving the finished bread a better taste. It's important to abide by the use-by date on the package but the good news is that it will keep for up to six months in the freezer and because it doesn't cake or stick together, can be used from frozen.

Bread the basic method

Once you've mastered the basic technique of kneading bread dough, the only limit is your imagination. Adding flavors, varying the texture, and shape are all variants on this basic method. See the recipe on page 18 for ingredients to prepare the basic bread dough.

The most critical stage in the bread-making process is the kneading, as it is during this process that the gluten in the flour is activated. The gluten develops further during rising, which is what gives the bread its finished texture.

step 1 Make a well in the center of the flour mixture and pour in the water. Mix to a dough, starting off with a wooden spoon and bringing the dough together with your hands.

step 2 Turn the dough onto a lightly floured surface. The texture will be very rough and slightly sticky. Begin kneading by folding the dough over itself and giving the dough a quarter turn.

step 3 Carry on kneading the dough for about 8–10 minutes until it is very smooth and elastic and no longer sticky. Alternatively, knead the dough on a mixer fitted with a dough hook for 6–8 minutes.

step 4 Lightly grease a large bowl. Form the dough into a neat ball and drop the dough carefully into the bowl. Rub a little oil over the surface of the dough, or use an oil mister and spray lightly. Cover with plastic wrap and leave to rise at room temperature for 1 hour or until doubled in bulk.

step 5 After about an hour, the dough will have risen nearly to the top of the bowl. Remove the plastic wrap and tip the dough onto a lightly floured surface. This will knock the dough back. Knead for an additional 2–3 minutes until smooth again.

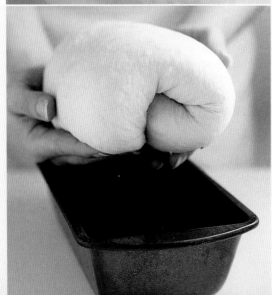

step 6 To shape the dough, pat into a large oblong. Fold one end to the center then fold the other end on top. Drop the dough into the prepared tin, seam-side down.

Basic white loaf

4½ cups white bread flour, plus extra for dusting • 1 tbsp. butter • 1 tbsp. salt •
2 tsp. instant yeast • a scant 2 cups lukewarm water • oil for greasing, an oil mister is
preferable

MAKES 1 large or 2 small loaves

**This is a simple, basic white loaf recipe—the kind you can
whip up when you get home from work, if you feel so
inclined. The longer and slower the proving, however, as
with all breads, the better the flavor will be.**

1. Generously grease either one 2-lb. loaf pan or two 1-lb. loaf
pans. Sift the flour into a large bowl. Rub the butter into the flour
until combined. Stir the salt and yeast into the flour.

2. Follow steps 1–6 in the basic method (pages 16–17), dividing
the dough in two before shaping, if making two small loaves.

3. Sprinkle the top of the dough with a dusting of flour then set the
pan or pans aside in an oiled plastic bag until the dough rises to the
top of the pan. This will take 30 minutes to 1 hour, depending on
the room temperature. Meanwhile, preheat the oven to 450° F.

4. Just before baking, make a slash down the length of the dough
with a sharp knife or scalpel. Transfer the loaf or loaves to the
preheated oven and bake for 40–45 minutes for the large single
loaf and 35–40 minutes for the two smaller loaves. The bread is
cooked when it is a rich golden brown and sounds hollow when
tapped on the bottom. Remove from the pans and return to the
oven to crisp the sides and base, about 5 minutes. Let cool
completely before serving.

Basic whole-wheat loaf

3 cups whole-wheat bread flour, plus extra for dusting • 2 tsp. salt • 1 tsp. brown sugar • 2 tsp. instant yeast • about 1½ cups lukewarm water • a little oil for greasing

MAKES 1 large or 2 small loaves

If you prefer, substitute half the whole-wheat flour with malted grain flour or white bread flour in this recipe.

1. Generously grease either one 2-lb. loaf pan or two 1-lb. loaf pans. Mix together the flour, salt, sugar, and yeast.

2. Follow step 1 in the basic method (see pages 16–17), adding a little more or less water as necessary (whole-wheat bread flour varies enormously in its absorption). Continue following steps 2 and 3 in the basic method, kneading only for 3–4 minutes until smooth. Then proceed to step 6. This bread does not require extensive kneading. Fit the dough into the pan or pans, pressing around the edges so that the top will be slightly rounded.

3. Dust the top of the loaf or loaves with extra flour then transfer to an oiled polythene bag. Leave to rise for about 30–45 minutes or until the dough reaches the top of the pan. Meanwhile, preheat the oven to 400° F.

4. Bake 20–25 minutes for the smaller breads or 30–35 minutes for the larger size.

5. Turn out of the pan and return to the oven, upside down until the sides and bottom are crisp, about 5–10 minutes. Check that the loaf is cooked by tapping the bottom. It should sound hollow. Cool the bread on a wire rack before slicing.

Bread rolls

1 quantity of any of the following doughs • baguette (see page 26) • spiced potato bread (see page 29) • malted grain, walnut and raisin loaf (see page 22) • millet, cheese, and caraway loaf (see page 24) • rye bread (see page 47) • rosemary, walnut, and tomato bread (see page 49)

Toppings • sesame seeds • poppy seeds • pumpkin seeds • mixed seeds, e.g., caraway, fennel and poppy • finely sliced onion • shredded cheese

THE NUMBER OF ROLLS will vary depending on the dough recipe used

These are fairly large crusty rolls, suitable for sandwiches, but also great with homemade soups.

1. Make your chosen dough up to the point at which it is shaped. Divide the dough into pieces each weighing about 2 oz. (the number of pieces will vary depending on the recipe). Cover the pieces you are not using with plastic wrap or a clean damp dishtowel.

2. To shape the dough, flour your hands and, working on a floured surface, form a piece of dough into an oval. Gently roll the dough using the palms of your hands making each end narrower than the middle, then twist each end into a point. Repeat to make all the rolls.

3. Transfer the formed rolls to a floured dishtowel, cover with another dishtowel and leave to rise until doubled in size, about 30 minutes to 1 hour.

4. Brush the tops of the rolls lightly with water and sprinkle over the topping of your choice. Transfer to a lightly oiled baking tray.

5. Bake at the temperature recommended in the dough recipe, testing that the rolls are cooked by tapping on the bottom, about 15–20 minutes. They are cooked when they sound hollow.

Malted grain, hazelnut, and raisin loaf

3 ⅓ cups malted grain bread flour, plus extra for dusting • 1 tsp. salt • 2 tbsp. butter, diced • 2 tbsp. brown sugar • 1 tbsp. instant yeast • 1 cup jumbo oats, plus extra for sprinkling • 1 ¼ cups lukewarm water • ⅓ cup hazelnuts, roughly chopped • ⅓ cup raisins • vegetable oil, for greasing

MAKES 1 large loaf

This is a fabulous bread—full of flavor and texture—and there's no need to bake it in a pan.

1. Mix the flour and salt in a large bowl. Rub the butter into the flour until combined. Stir the sugar, yeast, and oats into the flour and stir well to mix.

2. Follow steps 1–5 in the basic method (see pages 16–17), leaving the dough to rise until doubled in size, 45 minutes. Turn the dough onto a clean surface. Sprinkle the dough with nuts and raisins and knead well until incorporated (see upper right).

3. Lightly oil a large baking sheet and line with waxed paper. Shape the dough into a neat oval and place on the prepared baking sheet (see lower right). Press any raisins on the surface into the dough or they'll burn. Cover with an oiled plastic bag and leave to rise until doubled in size, 20–30 minutes.

4. Meanwhile, preheat the oven to 425° F. Remove the bag and brush the top of the bread with a little water. Sprinkle with a few extra oats. Using a sharp knife or scalpel, make several angled slashes across the top of the dough.

5. Transfer the baking sheet to the oven and bake until well-risen and golden and the loaf sounds hollow when tapped on the bottom, 35–40 minutes. Cool completely on a wire rack before serving.

Millet, cheese, and caraway loaf

1 ½ cups white bread flour • 1 ½ cups whole-wheat bread flour • 1 tbsp. brown sugar •
2 tsp. instant yeast • ½ cup lukewarm water • ⅕ cup whole millet • ½ cup boiling water •
2 tsp. salt • 1 tsp. caraway seeds • ⅔ cup grated strong cheddar cheese • vegetable oil
for greasing

MAKES 1 small loaf

This bread involves making a starter "sponge"—the extra
rising helps to add flavor to the bread. Buy millet from
health food shops.

1. Lightly grease a 2-lb. loaf pan. Set aside. In a large bowl, mix
together ⅓ cup of both the white and brown flour, the sugar, yeast,
and water to make a smooth batter. Cover and set aside in a warm
place until doubled in size, about 40 minutes.

2. Cover the millet with the boiling water. Leave to soak for 20
minutes.

3. Stir in the remaining flour, millet, and any water remaining, salt,
cumin, and cheese. Mix together well, with a little extra water if
necessary to form a stiff dough.

4. Follow steps 2–5 in the basic method (see pages 16–17),
leaving the dough to rise about 1–1 ½ hours or until doubled.

5. Shape the dough following step 6 (see pages 16–17). Cover the
pan with oiled plastic wrap. Leave to rise until the dough reaches
the top of the pan, about 30–40 minutes.

6. Meanwhile, preheat the oven to 450° F. Uncover the pan,
transfer it to the oven, and bake until risen and golden, 35–40
minutes. The bread should sound hollow when tapped on the
bottom. Let cool completely before serving.

Pesto bread

1 tbsp. instant yeast • 2½ cups lukewarm water • 4½ cups white bread flour, plus extra for dusting • 1 tbsp. salt • 1 tsp. sugar • 6 tbsp. olive oil, plus extra for greasing • 2 garlic cloves, minced • handful basil leaves, finely chopped

MAKES 1 loaf

1. Whisk the yeast and warm water together until the yeast has dissolved. Stir in half the flour until smooth. Cover and set aside in a warm place until the "sponge" has risen by about one-third and is clearly active with lots of bubbles, about 1 hour.

2. Mix the remaining flour with the "sponge," salt, sugar, and 2 tbsp. of oil. Mix to a soft dough.

3. Follow steps 2–5 of the basic white method (see pages 16–17), leaving the dough to rise until doubled in size, about 1–2½ hours.

4. Mix the remaining oil, garlic, and basil. Season and set aside.

5. Line a baking sheet with waxed paper. Lightly grease the paper. Turn the dough onto a floured surface. Knead for 1–2 minutes, then divide the dough in two. Shape into a large rectangle, 9 x 16 inches. Spread with the basil mixture.

6. Fold one long side of the dough over to fold in half. Cover with a clean dishtowel and leave to rise, about 30 minutes.

7. Meanwhile, preheat the oven to 475° F. Transfer the baking sheet to the oven and bake for 10 minutes. Reduce the oven temperature to 400° F and bake an additional 15 minutes until well risen and golden. Remove from the oven and cover with a clean dishtowel. Leave until cold.

Baguette

3 cups all-purpose flour • 3 cups white bread flour • 2 heaping tsp. salt • 1 tsp. golden brown sugar • 1 ½ tsp. instant yeast • 2 ½ cups cool water • vegetable oil, an oil mister is preferable • a little semolina for dusting • water in a mister   **MAKES 3 baguettes**

1. Mix the flours, salt, sugar, and yeast together. Follow steps 1-5 in the basic method (see pages 16–17), leaving the dough to rise for just 30 minutes.

2. Knead the dough 30 seconds, then shape into a ball. Return to the bowl, cover, and leave to rise until doubled in size, 1 ½ hours. Divide the dough into three pieces and shape into ovals. Cover with a damp dishtowel or plastic wrap and leave to rest, 10 minutes.

3. Shape the dough, one piece at a time. Place smooth side down on a lightly floured work surface. Flatten slightly with floured hands. Fold the top edge of the dough to the center and fold the bottom edge up to meet it. Press down with your fingertips. Follow steps **a**, **b**, and **c** (see right). Cover with a damp dishtowel. Leave until doubled in size, about 2 hours.

4. Preheat the oven to 500° F. Put a pizza stone or heavy baking tray on a central rack. On another baking tray, scatter some semolina, and using the cloth to help you, roll the first loaf, top side down onto the tray. Using a sharp knife or scalpel, slash the dough at an angle at regular intervals. Repeat with all three loaves.

5. Transfer the tray to the oven so that it sits on the pizza stone or heavy baking tray. Working quickly, spray the oven and the bread with water from the mister. Close the oven door. Spray again after 2–3 minutes, then lower the oven temperature to 450° F.

6. Cook until the crust is golden and the loaves sound hollow when tapped, 20–25 minutes. Leave until just warm or completely cold.

step a Using the index finger of one hand, press down on the center of the dough. Pinch the dough round your finger, using your other hand.

step b Gently roll the dough backwards and forwards until the sausage of dough is an even shape.

step c Lightly flour a clean dishtowel and lay onto a baking sheet. Pull up at 2 inch intervals to form tunnels. Transfer the shaped dough to the dishtowel, seam side up.

Soda bread

2 ¼ cups whole-wheat flour • ¾ cup all-purpose flour • 1 tsp. salt • 2 tsp. baking soda • 2 tbsp. butter • 1 ¼ cups buttermilk

MAKES 1 loaf

Soda bread makes an excellent accompaniment to hearty soups and is very quick to make. It is best eaten on the day it is made, but it toasts well on day two.

1. Preheat the oven to 400° F. Lightly grease a baking sheet.

2. Sift together the flours, salt, and baking soda. Rub in the butter, then stir in most of the buttermilk—you may need more or less depending on the flour. The dough will be quite lumpy at this stage.

3. Turn the dough onto a floured surface and knead until smooth and slightly sticky, about 3 minutes. Shape into a lightly flattened ball about 8 inches in diameter. Transfer to the baking sheet.

4. Using a sharp knife, cut a deep cross in the top of the loaf, without cutting all the way through. Transfer to the center of the oven.

5. Cook until the bread is deep golden and sounds hollow when tapped on the bottom, 30–35 minutes. Cover with foil after about 20 minutes if the bread begins to overbrown. Eat warm or cold.

Spiced potato bread

¾ cup plus 2 tbsp. all-purpose flour • 1¾ cups strong white bread flour •
½ cup cooked potato, mashed • 1 tsp. salt • ½ tsp. soft light brown sugar •
¾ tsp. instant yeast • 1 tsp. cumin seeds, lightly crushed • 1¼ cups cool water •
vegetable oil, an oil mister is preferable   **MAKES 1 loaf**

This unusual dough looks quite rustic and has a lovely chewy crust. Excellent with soup or toasted with butter.

1. Mix together the flours, potato, salt, sugar, yeast, and cumin seeds. Add the water and mix to a very soft and sticky dough.

2. Using a mixer fitted with a dough hook, knead the dough for about 6–7 minutes until very smooth and sticky. Scrape the dough into a clean bowl, cover and leave to rise until doubled, about 45 minutes to 1 hour.

3. Cover a baking sheet with waxed paper and generously flour the paper. Scrape the bread dough onto the paper, spray lightly with vegetable oil, and cover loosely with plastic wrap. Leave to rise until doubled, about 1 hour.

4. Meanwhile preheat the oven to 475° F. Put a heavy baking sheet upside down on the center shelf while the oven is preheating. Put an empty shallow roasting tray in the bottom of the oven. Uncover the bread and transfer it to the baking sheet in the oven, paper and all. Quickly pour 2 cups of water into the roasting tray and spray the oven walls and bread with water. Reduce the oven to 450° F. Cook for 20 minutes until the bread is well colored and sounds hollow when tapped on the bottom. Allow to cool on a wire rack.

Bagels

1 ¼ cups lukewarm water • 2 tsp. instant yeast • 4 ½ cups white bread flour • 2 tsp. salt • 1 ½ tbsp. honey or 1 tbsp. malt syrup • cornmeal for dusting

MAKES 8 bagels

This makes quite a stiff dough, so if you are planning to knead using a machine, be careful as stiff doughs can be very hard on mixer motors. If your machine struggles, you may have to knead by hand.

1. Mix the water and yeast together and leave until the yeast has dissolved, about 3 minutes.

2. Add a scant 2 cups of the flour and stir well to make a thick batter. Set aside in a warm place until doubled in bulk and obviously active with lots of bubbles, about 1 hour.

3. Add the remaining flour, salt, and honey or malt syrup and mix to a stiff dough. Turn the dough onto a lightly floured surface and knead until dense and dry, 12–15 minutes. If using a machine, mix for 1 minute on a low speed until everything is combined, then knead for on a medium speed (see introductory note above), 10–12 minutes. You may need to add a little more flour or water to achieve the right texture.

4. Cut the dough into eight equal pieces and roll into balls. Cover with plastic wrap or a clean dishtowel and leave to rest for 5 minutes.

5. Line a baking sheet with waxed paper and dust liberally with cornmeal. Follow steps **a** and **b** (right).

6. Put the formed bagels about 2 inches apart on the prepared baking sheet, enclose everything in an oiled plastic bag and leave to rise for about 1½ hours until increased in size by about twenty-five percent (this is a dense dough which will not rise as quickly as some lighter doughs).

7. The bagels can be cooked immediately, but they will improve if chilled at least 6 hours or overnight. Remove from the fridge 1 hour before cooking.

8. When ready to cook the bagels, preheat the oven to 475° F. Fill a large pan with at least 4 inches of water and bring to a boil. Reduce the heat to a gentle simmer. Working in batches, gently drop the bagels into the water. Do not crowd the pan.

9. After 1 minute, flip the bagels and poach for an additional 1 minute. Drain with a slotted spoon and place 2 inches apart on a clean baking sheet, lined and dusted with cornmeal, as before.

10. Bake until golden brown, 10–12 minutes, rotating the pan halfway through to ensure they're evenly cooked. Cool on a wire rack.

step a Poke a hole right through the center of each piece of dough with your index finger. Repeat to make holes in all the balls of dough.

step b Pick up a ball of dough and put your index fingers through the hole from each side. Turn the dough over and over to expand the hole to about 1½ inches.

English muffins

3½ cups white bread flour, plus a little extra for dusting • 2 tsp. instant yeast • 1 tsp. sugar • 1½ tsp. salt • 1 cup lukewarm milk • 4 tbsp. hand-hot water • a little vegetable shortening or oil

MAKES 12 muffins

Unusually, these little buns are cooked on the stove. If you don't have a griddle, use a heavy skillet.

1. Mix together the flour, yeast, sugar and salt. Follow steps 1–5 in the basic method (see pages 16–17), using the milk and water to make the dough in step 1.

2. Tip the dough onto a lightly floured surface and roll it out to about ½-inch thick. Using a plain 4-inch biscuit cutter, cut out twelve rounds, rerolling the dough as necessary.

3. Put the muffins on an ungreased, lightly floured baking sheet, and sprinkle them with a little more flour. Cover loosely with a plastic bag and leave to rise again in a warm place, about 25–35 minutes.

4. Lightly grease a griddle or heavy skillet with a little vegetable shortening or oil. Put the pan over a medium heat and when hot, add 3 or 4 muffins (do not overcrowd the pan). Reduce the heat to low and cook for about 7 minutes on each side until golden. Cook the remaining muffins in the same way.

5. To serve, break the muffins open around the center and toast. Butter generously and serve.

Hazelnut and apricot dinner rolls

4 tsp. instant yeast • 2 tbsp. honey • 2⅔ cups lukewarm water • 3 cups white bread flour, plus extra for dusting • 2½ cups semolina flour, plus extra for dusting • 2 tsp. salt • ⅓ cup blanched hazelnuts • ¼ cup roughly chopped semidried apricots

MAKES 8 rolls

Although these rolls are reasonably substantial, they make an excellent accompaniment to salad at the beginning or middle of a meal.

1. Dissolve the yeast with the honey in the tepid water. Mix together the flours and salt in a large bowl. Make a well in the center and add the yeast mixture. Mix together to form a soft dough.

2. Follow steps 2–5 in the basic method (see pages 16–17).

3. Meanwhile, preheat the oven to 425° F. Toast the hazelnuts, watching them carefully, until golden and aromatic, 3–5 minutes. Leave until cool enough to handle, then roughly chop. Lightly grease a 9-inch springform pan.

4. Turn the dough onto a clean surface and knead in the chopped hazelnuts and apricots. Break the dough into eight equal-sized pieces. Shape into balls and arrange in the pan, seven around the edge and one in the middle. Cover with oiled plastic wrap and leave to rise until doubled in size, 40 minutes to 1 hour.

5. Transfer to the oven and cook until golden, 25–30 minutes. Tap the bottom to check if the bread is done. If it sounds hollow, it is cooked, otherwise return it to the oven for an additional 5–10 minutes.

6. Let cool on a wire rack, then unmold and break into individual rolls.

Foccacia

1 tbsp. instant yeast • 2¾ cups lukewarm water • 6 cups white bread flour, plus extra for dusting • 1 tbsp. salt • 1 tsp. sugar • 1 tbsp. olive oil, plus extra for brushing • 2 large sprigs fresh rosemary, leaves only, roughly chopped • 6 tbsp. extra-virgin olive oil • 2 tsp. coarse sea salt   **MAKES 2 loaves**

Experiment with different toppings—finely sliced onions, garlic, pitted olives, and chopped sundried tomatoes are all excellent. This bread is made from a very sticky dough which really must be kneaded by machine.

1. Whisk together the yeast and the water until the yeast has dissolved. Stir in half the flour until smooth. Cover and set aside in a warm place until the "sponge" has risen by about one third and is clearly active with lots of bubbles, 1½–2 hours.

2. Put the remaining flour in the bowl of a mixer fitted with a dough hook and add the "sponge," salt, sugar, and olive oil. Mix at the lowest speed until firm but still sticking to the bowl, 7 minutes. Add more flour or water as necessary.

3. Increase the speed to high and knead for 1 minute more until the dough is elastic and springs back when pushed with a finger.

4. Follow steps 4 and 5 in the basic method (see pages 16–17), and leave the dough to rise until doubled in size, 1½–2 hours.

5. Turn the dough, which will be sticky, onto a well-floured surface. Flour your hands and tap out into a rough rectangle. Fold in half, then in three in the opposite direction. Divide the dough in two and tap each piece into a rectangle again. Transfer to two floured nonstick 9- x 13- x 1-inch pans, pushing the dough to fill the pans evenly.

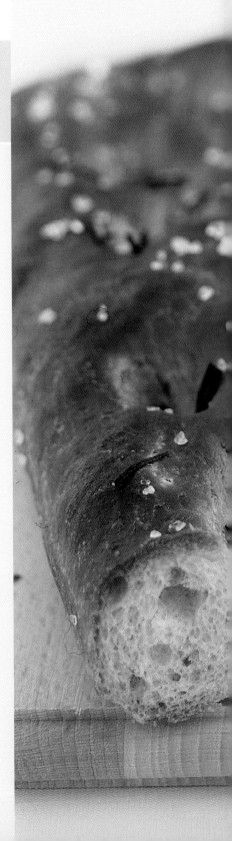

6. Cover both loaves with a dishtowel and leave to rise, about 1 hour. Meanwhile, preheat the oven to 475° F.

7. Using the tips of your fingers or the handle of a wooden spoon, poke holes in the dough all over. Sprinkle on the rosemary, then drizzle with the extra-virgin olive oil. Scatter over the coarse salt.

8. Bake in the center of the oven, 10 minutes. Reduce the heat to 400° F and cook until golden and risen, 15–20 minutes. Let cool in the pans before serving.

Ciabatta

3 cups white bread flour, plus extra for dusting • ½ tsp. instant yeast • 1¾ cups lukewarm water • ½ tsp. brown sugar • 1½ tsp. salt • 2 tbsp. extra virgin olive oil • vegetable or olive oil, for greasing • semolina, for dusting • water, in a mister

MAKES 2 loaves

Ciabatta is another very wet, rustic style bread that needs to be kneaded using a machine. You will need to start making this bread the day before you intend to bake it.

1. To make the "sponge," mix together half the flour with half the yeast and the water. Whisk until smooth. Set aside until doubled in size and very foamy, about 1–2 hours.

2. In the bowl of a mixer fitted with a dough hook, mix together the remaining flour and yeast, olive oil, sugar, salt, and "sponge." You may need to scrape down the sides occasionally using a wet spatula.

3. Mix on a medium speed, about 7 minutes. The dough will be very wet and stretchy. If not, add a few drops of water.

4. Using a wet spatula, scrape the dough down into a rough mass. Cover and leave to stand at room temperature, about 3 hours. It will rise very slowly. Transfer to the refrigerator and leave overnight.

5. Line two baking sheets with waxed paper. Brush lightly with oil, then sprinkle generously with semolina.

6. Dip your hands in some water and then transfer the dough to a clean surface. Sprinkle the dough generously with flour. Dip a knife in water and cut the dough in two equal pieces. Now flour your hands and lift each of the pieces, stretching to about 12 inches, and lay each on its own sheet. The dough may shrink back but should remain oblong. Stretch the dough a little if necessary.

7. Enclose each baking sheet in an oiled plastic bag and leave to rise at room temperature until doubled in size, about 2 hours.

8. Meanwhile, preheat the oven to 500° F or its highest setting, whichever is hotter. Put a shallow roasting tray or ovenproof skillet in the bottom of the oven. Put a pizza stone or heavy baking sheet on the center shelf.

9. Slide the baking sheets out of their bags and burst any noticeable air pockets in the dough. Slide the dough, paper, and all, onto the pizza stone or baking sheet. Spray the oven and breads with water and pour 2 cups of water into the roasting tray or skillet. Shut the door quickly. Wait 2–3 minutes, then spray the oven again. Reduce the temperature to 450° F and bake until the crust is a deep brown, 20–25 minutes.

10. Turn the oven off and open the door slightly. Leave the bread in the oven for an additional 5–10 minutes, allowing it to finish cooking without burning. Remove the waxed paper and cool on a wire rack.

Pretzels

3 cups all-purpose flour • 1 cup strong white bread flour extra bread flour • 2½ tsp. instant yeast • 2 tbsp. soft light brown sugar • 1 heaped tsp. salt • ½ cups warm water • 2 tbsp. baking soda • 2 tbsp. kosher sea salt • vegetable oil, an oil mister is preferable

MAKES 12 pretzels

These are large, soft pretzels. Sprinkle with sesame seeds or poppy seeds if you prefer. Eat them on the day they are baked.

1. Mix together the flours, yeast, sugar and salt in a large mixing bowl. Add the water and mix to a soft dough. Knead for about 5 minutes until smooth and elastic. Shape into a neat ball and put into an oiled bowl. Lightly oil the surface of the dough and cover the bowl with plastic wrap. Leave to rise 1 hour, or until doubled in bulk.

2. Cover 2 large cookie sheets with waxed paper and set aside. Preheat the oven to 450° F.

3. Cut the dough into 12 equal pieces. Take the first piece and roll it using the palms of your hands into a long thin rope, about as thin as a pencil. Shape into a pretzel by crossing over the ends, twisting them, then folding them up over the loop. Set aside on a floured surface. Shape all the pretzels.

4. Mix the baking soda with about 2 cups hand-hot water until dissolved. Dip the pretzels, one at a time, into the solution then transfer to the prepared cookie sheets, leaving them well-spaced. Sprinkle with the kosher salt. Leave to rise, 15–20 minutes until just puffed up. Bake 8–10 minutes until golden. Serve warm or cold.

Pooris

¾ cup whole-wheat flour • ¾ cup all-purpose flour • 2 tsp. salt • 2 tbsp. vegetable oil, plus more for frying the pooris • scant ½ cup water

MAKES 12 pooris

1. Mix the two flours with the salt. Drizzle over the oil and rub it in with your fingertips until the mixture resembles coarse bread crumbs.

2. Gradually add enough of the water to form a stiff dough. Turn the dough onto a clean surface and knead until smooth, 10–12 minutes.

3. Form the dough into a ball and rub the surface with a little oil. Put into a clean bowl and cover with plastic wrap. Leave for 30 minutes.

4. Knead the dough briefly and then divide into twelve equal balls. Cover with a clean damp dishtowel. Form the pooris by rolling each ball into a 5-inch circle. If possible, roll out all the pooris before cooking and keep them covered with plastic wrap. If space is at a premium, you may need to work in batches.

5. When ready to cook, heat about 1-inch of oil over a medium heat in a deep skillet large enough to hold one poori comfortably. Let the oil get very hot. Meanwhile, line a plate with paper towels.

6. Lift one poori and lay it carefully in the hot oil. It'll sink, then rise immediately and begin sizzling. Using the back of a large spoon or tongs, push the poori into the oil. After a few seconds, when the poori has puffed up, turn it over and cook an additional 10 seconds, until golden and covered in puffed "bubbles." Drain on paper towels. Cook all the pooris this way, layering them with paper towels, if necessary. Serve hot.

Chapatis

scant 2 cups whole-wheat or chapati flour, plus extra for dusting • 1 tsp. salt • generous ½ cup lukewarm water • melted butter or ghee for brushing (optional)

MAKES 8 chapatis

1. If using whole-wheat flour, sift to remove the bran. Stir the salt into the flour. Gradually add the water and mix to form a soft dough.

2. Knead until smooth, 6–8 minutes, adding a little flour if necessary. Form into a ball and put into a clean bowl. Cover with plastic wrap and leave to rest, 30 minutes.

3. Knead the dough again briefly, then divide into eight equal balls. Cover with a clean damp dishtowel. With floured hands, take one ball of dough and, on a lightly floured surface, roll it into a 6-inch circle, dusting often with flour to prevent sticking. Repeat to make all the chapatis.

4. Meanwhile, heat a heavy-based skillet over a medium heat until very hot. Shake any excess flour off and put a chapati into the dry skillet. Cook for about 30 seconds to 1 minute, until starting to color. Turn and cook for an additional 30 seconds to 1 minute on the second side. If using, brush with melted butter or ghee and flip again to puff the chapati. Put on a plate lined with a clean dry dishtowel. Repeat to make all the chapatis.

5. Eat straight away, or stack and wrap in foil, then freeze. Reheat, wrapped in the foil, at 425° F, 15–20 minutes.

Naan

2¼ cups self-rising flour • 1 tsp. salt • 2 tbsp. plain yogurt • ½ cup lukewarm water • melted butter or ghee, for brushing (optional)

MAKES 4 naan breads

This bread is traditionally cooked on the walls of a tandoor, a large clay oven capable of very high temperatures. The only way to approximate this type of cooking at home is to use a very hot broiler.

1. Sift the flour and salt into a bowl. Whisk the yogurt into the water. Make a well in the center of the flour, pour in the liquid and mix to a soft dough. Turn onto a floured surface and knead until smooth, about 5 minutes.

2. Form into a ball and put into an oiled bowl. Cover with plastic wrap and leave to rest, 30 minutes.

3. Preheat the broiler to high. Divide dough into four and roll each piece into an oval about 8 inches long. Broil each bread until puffed up and speckled brown, 1–2 minutes each side. Brush with the melted butter or ghee, if using. Serve warm.

Pita

3 cups white bread flour • 1 tsp. salt • 2 tsp. instant yeast • 2 tbsp. olive oil • 1 ½ cups cool water

MAKES 8 pita breads

You will get the best results from this dough if you use a pizza stone to cook them on. Make sure you leave enough headroom in the oven for the breads to puff up, otherwise they may burn if they touch the top of the oven or any of the oven shelves.

1. Mix all the ingredients together until they form a ball. Tip onto a lightly floured surface and knead, 12–15 minutes. Alternatively, mix the ingredients in a mixer, fitted with a dough hook, and knead on slow speed, about 10 minutes.

2. Put the dough into a lightly oiled bowl, oil the surface lightly, and cover with plastic wrap. Leave until doubled in size, 1 ½ hours.

3. Put a pizza stone or upturned heavy baking sheet in the top one third of the oven and preheat to 475° F. Divide the dough into eight equal pieces. Roll each piece into a ball and flatten into a disk. Cover the disks with plastic wrap and let rest, 20 minutes.

4. Roll the dough into rounds or oblongs about ¼ inch thick. Leave to rest, uncovered, before cooking, 10 minutes.

5. Spray the pizza stone lightly with water and place as many pitas on it as will fit without overlapping. Lower the oven temperature to 450° F and bake until they puff up, 3 minutes. Do not wait for them to brown or they will be too crisp. Remove from the oven and leave to cool on a wire rack. Repeat to cook all the pitas.

Pizza

1 ½ cups white bread flour • ½ tsp. salt • ½ tsp. instant yeast • ½ cup lukewarm water • 1 tbsp. olive oil • 1 lb. mixed fresh tomatoes, e.g., plum, beefsteak, red, yellow, and orange cherry tomatoes, sliced • 7 oz. mozzarella in brine, drained and broken into small pieces • handful basil leaves, roughly torn • extra-virgin olive oil for drizzling • semolina flour for dusting

MAKES two 9-inch pizzas

1. Mix the flour, salt, and yeast. Stir in the water and olive oil and mix to a soft dough. Follow steps 2–5 of the basic method (see pages 16–17).

2. Lay the tomato slices onto a double thickness of paper towels and leave to drain. Do the same with the mozzarella, covering with more paper towels and pressing down well to soak up the excess moisture. Preheat the oven to 500° F or its highest setting, whichever is hotter. Put a pizza stone or heavy baking sheet on the highest shelf.

3. Divide the dough in two and follow steps **a** and **b** (see below). Divide the tomatoes between pizza bases, leaving a rim of about ¾ inch. Sprinkle with cheese and basil. Season and drizzle with oil.

4. Carefully slide the pizzas from the baking sheet onto the hot baking sheet or pizza stone, and bake 12–15 minutes until golden.

step a Using wet hands, stretch the dough into a rough circle about 9 inches in diameter. Leave to rest for about 5 minutes.

step b Transfer the dough to a baking sheet, dusted generously with semolina, and continue shaping until about 10 inches in diameter, with a slightly raised edge.

Quattro formaggi pizza with walnuts

2 garlic cloves, minced • 4 tbsp. olive oil • 1 quantity pizza dough, ready for topping (see page 44) • 2 large tomatoes, thinly sliced • 2 tsp. chopped fresh oregano • 2 tbsp. chopped walnuts • 5 oz. mozzarella in brine, drained and broken into small pieces • 2 oz. Dolcelatte, crumbled • 4 tbsp. grated Parmesan • 5 oz. Fontina, sliced

MAKES two 9-inch pizzas

1. Mix together the garlic and olive oil and set aside. Preheat the oven to 500° F or its highest setting, whichever is hotter. Put a pizza stone or heavy baking sheet on the highest shelf.

2. Brush the prepared pizza bases with the garlic and oil mixture. Top with the tomatoes, oregano, walnuts, and then the cheeses. Season well and drizzle with any remaining garlic oil.

3. Transfer to the top of the oven and cook until the edges are browned, and the cheese is melted and bubbling, 10–12 minutes. Let cool for a few minutes before serving.

Roasted onion and goat cheese pizza

1 quantity pizza dough, ready for topping (see page 44) • 4 red onions • 2 tbsp. olive oil, plus extra for drizzling • 4 tbsp. tapenade or black olive paste • 4 oz. thinly sliced prosciutto, roughly torn • 4 oz. sundried tomatoes • 1 tbsp. fresh thyme leaves • ½ lb. rinded goats cheese, thinly sliced

MAKES two 9-inch pizzas

1. Preheat the broiler to high. Peel the onions, trimming but leaving the root end intact. Cut the onions into sixteen wedges through the root. Brush with olive oil and arrange in a broiler pan. Cook, turning once, until golden and tender, 6–8 minutes. Remove and set aside.

2. Preheat the oven to 500° F. Put a pizza stone or heavy baking sheet on the highest shelf.

3. Spread the pizzas with tapenade and divide the prosciutto between them. Scatter the sundried tomatoes and onions on top. Sprinkle with the thyme, and top with the cheese slices. Season well and drizzle with a little olive oil.

4. Transfer to the top of the oven and cook until golden and the cheese is bubbling, 10–12 minutes.

Rye bread

For the "sponge" • scant 1 cup white bread flour • scant 1 cup rye flour • 1 tsp. instant yeast • 1 cup cool water
For the bread • scant 2 cups white bread flour • 1 tbsp. golden brown sugar • 1 heaped tsp. salt • ½ tsp. instant yeast • 1½ tbsp. caraway seeds • 4 tbsp. buttermilk • vegetable oil, an oil mister is preferable   **MAKES 1 loaf**

This is quite a pale rye bread. You could substitute whole-wheat bread flour for the white flour, but you would need to increase the yeast to 2 tsp.

1. Combine all the "sponge" ingredients in a mixing bowl. Stir well to form a smooth, thick paste. Cover the bowl with plastic wrap and allow to rest at room temperature, until doubled in size, 4 hours.

2. Combine all the bread ingredients with the "sponge" in the same bowl and stir until they form a ball. Follow steps 4, 5, and 6 in the basic method (see pages 16–17), leaving the dough to rise until doubled in bulk, 90 minutes. Meanwhile, flour a baking sheet well.

3. Shape the dough into a neat oval and place on the prepared baking sheet. Rub or mist with vegetable oil and cover lightly with oiled plastic wrap. Leave to rise until doubled in size, 1–1½ hours.

4. Meanwhile, preheat the oven to 425° F. Put a heavy baking sheet upside down on the center shelf. Put an empty shallow roasting tray in the bottom of the oven.

5. Transfer the bread to the baking sheet in the oven by sliding it off the well-floured tray. Quickly pour a cup of water into the roasting tray and spray the walls of the oven and bread lightly with water. Close the door, wait 2–3 minutes, then spray again. Reduce the oven to 400° F and cook until well colored and the bread sounds hollow when tapped on the bottom, 35–40 minutes. Let cool on a wire rack.

Rosemary, walnut, and tomato bread

2 ⅓ cups whole-wheat or whole grain bread flour • 1 ½ tsp. instant yeast • scant 1 cup cool water • 2 tsp. salt • 2 tbsp. honey • 1 tbsp. finely chopped fresh rosemary • ⅓ cup walnut pieces, roughly chopped • 2 oz. semidried ("sunblush") tomatoes, drained and roughly chopped

MAKES 1 loaf

The advantage of making a "sponge" dough first, is that the bread has a much fuller flavor and a better texture. This is a beautifully colored bread with a fine texture. It is delicious with soups, but also makes a fabulous and unusual sandwich bread.

1. Mix about one-third of the flour with 1 tsp. of the yeast and the water. Mix to a thick paste, then cover the bowl with plastic wrap and leave to rise, about 4 hours, until well risen and very active.

2. Combine the remaining flour, yeast, salt, honey, rosemary, walnuts, and tomatoes with the "sponge" until the mixture forms a ball.

3. Follow step 3 from the basic method (see pages 16-17), kneading the dough for about 15 minutes, then follow steps 4 and 5 (see page 17), leaving the dough to rise about 1 ½ hours until doubled in size.

4. Shape the dough into a neat round and transfer to a baking sheet lined with waxed paper. Cover loosely with a clean dishtowel and let rise until doubled in size, 30–40 minutes.

5. Preheat the oven to 350° F. Bake the bread in the lower third of the oven, 20 minutes. Turn the bread and bake until the loaf sounds hollow when tapped on the bottom, a further 30–40 minutes. Cover with foil if it starts to overbrown. Let cool on a wire rack.

Croissants

3 cups white bread flour, plus extra for dredging • 1 tbsp. instant yeast • 1 tsp. salt • ⅓ cup sugar • ½ cup lukewarm water • ½ cup cold milk • 2 sticks plus 1 tbsp. unsalted butter • 1 egg yolk mixed with 1 tbsp. milk

MAKES 16 croissants

You need to start making these a day ahead of cooking them. It is well worth the effort, however, producing a crisp, flaky, buttery result. You may find using a mixer with a dough hook easier than kneading the rather sticky dough by hand. Leaving the dough to rest several times during rolling makes the job much easier.

1. Mix together the flour, yeast, salt, and sugar, preferably in a mixer fitted with a dough hook. Add the water and milk and mix on low speed until combined. Increase the speed to medium and work until the dough is soft and sticky, but coming away from the sides of the bowl, about 6 minutes. Scrape the dough into a plastic bag and chill overnight in the fridge.

2. Take the butter out of the fridge so that it is neither hard nor softened either. Put a sheet of plastic wrap on a clean surface and dredge with flour. Lay the butter on top. Sprinkle flour on the butter and then, using a rolling pin, knock it out into a rectangle about ½ inch thick. Wrap with the plastic wrap and return it to the fridge for a few minutes.

3. Take the dough out of the bag and put it on a floured surface. Scatter with more flour and roll out, turning frequently, into a rectangle about ½ inch thick. Brush off excess flour, then put the butter in the center. Fold the edges of the dough over the butter so that they overlap slightly to enclose the butter completely.

4. Scatter more flour over. Rolling away from you, roll the dough out into a long rectangle about 17 x 28 inches. Stop once or twice and leave the dough to rest for 5 minutes, then continue rolling. Fold one end in by a sixth and the other in by a sixth. Fold both ends over again by a sixth so that they meet in the center. Fold the two together, as if closing a book. Turn the dough so the fold is to one side. Roll it out away from you into a long rectangle as before and fold one end in by a quarter. Repeat at the other end so that they meet in the middle. Fold again as if closing a book. Seal the edges with pressure from the rolling pin. Wrap and chill 30 minutes to 1 hour.

5. Roll the dough on a floured surface to as neat a rectangle as possible, about 12 x 36 inches. Trim the edges straight, then cut in two lengthwise. Cut out eight equal triangles from each piece.

6. Lay the triangles, one at a time, with the point away from you. Roll up away from you finishing with the point underneath. Transfer to a lined baking tray, cover with plastic wrap and leave to rise until doubled in size, about 1–2 hours.

7. Meanwhile, preheat the oven to 400° F. Brush the egg and milk mixture lightly onto the dough, brushing from the middle outwards. Bake in the center of the oven, 10 minutes. Reduce the oven temperature to 325° F and bake until risen and golden, 20–25 minutes.

Caramel pecan loaf

3 cups white bread flour • 1 tbsp. butter • 2 tsp. salt • 1 ½ tsp. instant yeast • 1 ¼ cups lukewarm water • 1 ½ sticks unsalted butter • ⅔ cup golden brown sugar • ⅔ cup pecans, roughly chopped • 2 tbsp. heavy cream

MAKES 1 loaf

1. Generously grease a 9-inch springform cake pan and set aside. Sift the flour into a large bowl and add the butter. Rub the butter into the flour until combined. Follow steps 1–5 of the basic method (see pages 16–17).

2. Pat the dough out to a large 10- x 14-inch rectangle. Cover and let rest, 10 minutes.

3. Meanwhile, cream together 1 stick of the butter with ½ cup of the sugar until smooth. Stir in most of the pecans. Follow steps **a** and **b** (see right).

4. Cover the pan with a clean dishtowel and leave until the dough has risen to the top, about 30 minutes.

5. Preheat the oven to 400° F. Transfer the pan to the oven and bake until risen and golden, 30–40 minutes, covering the top with foil if it begins to overbrown.

6. Meanwhile, melt the remaining butter and sugar together over a low heat. Add the cream and bring to a boil. Simmer 3–4 minutes, then add the remaining pecans and cook another 1 minute. Remove from the heat.

7. Remove the bread from the oven and immediately spread the pecan mixture over the top. Let cool before serving.

step a Spread the pecan mixture evenly over the dough, leaving a 1-inch margin around the edges. Starting from a long side, roll the dough tightly into a sausage shape.

step b Cut the dough into 2-inch slices. Arrange the slices in the prepared pan, cut side up.

Danish pastries

1 quantity of croissant dough, prepared up to the end of step 4 (see pages 16–17) • 1 egg, beaten lightly with 1 tbsp. milk • 3 tbsp. apricot jelly • ½ cup confectioners' sugar • 1-2 tbsp. water or lemon juice
Cinnamon danish • 1 tsp. ground cinnamon • 1 tbsp. sugar
Pain aux raisins • ½ cup raisins
Fruit pinwheels • ½ cup almond paste • 6 canned apricot halves   MAKES 12–16 danish pastries

1. Roll the dough on a floured surface to a I-inch thick rectangle, about 36 x 12 inches. Trim and cut into three equal squares.

Cinnamon danish: mix cinnamon and sugar and sprinkle evenly over one square. Press lightly into the dough. Cut into 1-inch strips. Twist each strip, then coil the lengths into circles.

Pain aux raisins: sprinkle raisins over a second rectangle. Roll up from one short end. Cut into ½-inch thick slices.

Fruit pinwheels: cut the remaining rectangle into six squares. Divide almond paste into six and put in the center of the squares. Top with an apricot half. Make four diagonal cuts from each corner of the pastry as far as the edge of the apricot. Fold alternate points down to the center of the apricot.

2. When the pastries are shaped, lay well-spaced apart on a lined and greased baking sheet. Cover loosely with oiled plastic wrap and leave in a warm place until well risen, about 2 hours.

3. Preheat the oven to 350° F. Brush pastries with the egg and milk mixture and bake, 25–30 minutes. Melt and sieve apricot jelly and brush over the warm pastries. When cold, mix together the confectioners' sugar and water or lemon juice until you have a smooth, thick frosting. Drizzle over the pastries.

Cinnamon raisin bread

3½ cups white bread flour, plus extra for dusting • 1 tbsp. butter • 1 tbsp. salt • 2 tsp. instant yeast • 2 tsp. sugar • 1¼ cups lukewarm water • 1 tsp. cinnamon • ¼ cups light brown sugar • ½ cup raisins

MAKES 1 loaf

1. Generously grease a 2-lb. loaf pan. Sift the flour into a large bowl and add the butter. Rub the butter into the flour until combined.

2. Stir the salt, yeast, and sugar into the flour and stir well to mix.

3. Follow steps 1–5 in the basic method (see pages 16–17).

4. Tap the dough out into a large rectangle, cover, and leave to rest, 10 minutes.

5. Using a rolling pin, roll the dough into a rectangle measuring 14 x 10 inches. Mix the cinnamon, sugar, and raisins together and sprinkle evenly over the dough.

6. Starting from one short end, roll the dough, jelly roll style, to enclose the filling. Tuck the ends under a little to fit the pan, then place the dough seam side down in the pan. Cover with oiled plastic wrap and leave to rise to the top of the pan, about 30 minutes.

7. Meanwhile, preheat the oven to 425° F. Transfer the pan to the oven and bake until risen and golden, 35–40 minutes, covering with foil after 15–20 minutes if necessary. The bread is cooked when it is a rich golden brown and sounds hollow when tapped on the bottom. Let cool on a wire rack.

Doughnuts

1 tbsp. instant yeast • ¾ cup lukewarm milk • scant 1 ¼ cups all-purpose flour • 2 cups white bread flour, plus extra for kneading • 1 tsp. salt • 6 tbsp. unsalted butter, diced and softened • 2 medium eggs, beaten • ⅓ cup sugar, plus extra for coating • 2 tsp. grated lemon peel • 1 tsp. ground cinnamon • sunflower oil for brushing • oil for deep frying

MAKES about 20 doughnuts

1. Whisk yeast and milk to dissolve. Stir in the all-purpose flour. Cover bowl with plastic wrap. Leave until "sponge" has risen, 2 hours.

2. Put the bread flour in the bowl of a mixer fitted with a dough hook and add the "sponge" and salt. Turn on the machine at the lowest speed and begin adding the butter, one cube at a time. Then add the eggs, one at a time, then sugar and lemon peel. Knead for 8 minutes. Turn the speed to high and knead, 2 minutes.

3. Knead by hand on a floured surface, adding more flour, until elastic and smooth. Shape into a ball and put into a lightly oiled bowl. Lightly oil the top, cover, and leave until doubled in size, 2 hours.

4. Divide into twenty pieces and roll each into a neat ball. Make ring doughnuts by pressing your finger all the way through to make 1-inch holes, or leave whole. Put the doughnuts onto a floured tray and cover with a clean dishtowel. Leave to rise until doubled in size, 40–50 minutes.

5. Fill a large deep saucepan about one third with oil. Heat until the oil reaches 350° F or until a cube of bread browns in 50 seconds. Fry the doughnuts in small batches, taking care not to overcrowd the pan, turning them once until browned and puffed up, about 2–3 minutes. Drain on paper towels.

6. Mix extra sugar with the cinnamon on a plate and roll the doughnuts in the mixture while still warm. Serve as soon as possible.

Panettone

1 tbsp. instant yeast • generous ½ cup lukewarm milk • 2¾ cups all-purpose flour • 1 medium egg • 4 medium egg yolks • 2 tsp. salt • ⅔ cup sugar • 2 tsp. grated lemon peel • 2 tsp. grated orange peel • ⅔ cup unsalted butter, softened • ½ cup chopped mixed candied orange and citron peel • ¾ cup raisins

MAKES 1 large loaf

This bread dough takes time to rise. Don't leave it in a very warm place once the butter has been incorporated or it will melt and the dough will be greasy.

1. Line a 6-inch round cake pan (with a depth of 4 inches) with a double layer of waxed paper that is 5 inches higher than the rim of the pan. Dissolve the yeast in 4 tbsp. of the warm milk. Cover and leave in a warm place until frothy. Stir in ¾ cup of the flour and the remaining warm milk. Cover and leave to rise, about 30 minutes.

2. Beat together the egg and egg yolks. Sift the remaining flour and salt into the yeast mixture. Make a well in the center and add the sugar, eggs, and lemon and orange peel. Knead until elastic, about 5 minutes. Work in the butter until evenly incorporated.

3. Form into a ball and place in a clean bowl. Cover and leave in a cool place until doubled in size, 2–4 hours, the longer the better.

4. Preheat the oven to 400° F. Turn the dough onto a clean surface and knead in the candied peel and raisins. Form into a neat ball and place in the prepared pan. Cut a cross in the top with a sharp knife. Cover and leave to rise until the dough is 1 inch above the top of the pan.

5. Bake for 15 minutes, then lower the heat to 350° F and bake until well risen and golden, an additional 40 minutes. Leave in the pan for 10 minutes, then transfer to a wire rack to cool.

Scones

1½ cups all-purpose flour • 1 tsp. baking powder • ½ tsp. baking soda • pinch of salt • 1½ cups sugar • 1½ oz. unsalted butter, soft • ½ cup buttermilk • 1 tbsp. milk • 1 egg, beaten • 3 tbsp. coarse sugar

MAKES 6–8 scones

Although scone dough must be kneaded to bring it together, it is important not to overknead—this will make them tough, instead of light and flaky, as they should be.

1. Preheat the oven to 300° F. Line a baking sheet with waxed paper. Sift the flour, baking powder, baking soda, salt, and sugar into a large bowl.

2. Add the butter and rub into the flour mixture until it resembles coarse bread crumbs.

3. Stir in the buttermilk until the ingredients just form a ball, adding a little extra if needed.

4. Lightly flour a work surface and turn the dough onto it. Knead the dough briefly, then pat into a circle about 1 inch thick and about 6 inches in diameter. Cut the circle into six or eight wedges (you could use a biscuit cutter, but you will have to reroll the trimmings, possibly resulting in overworked dough).

5. Transfer the wedges to the prepared baking sheet. Lightly brush the top with a little milk, then sprinkle with the coarse sugar.

6. Transfer to the oven and bake until risen and golden, about 20–25 minutes.

7. Cool the scones on a wire rack about 10 minutes before serving.

Brioche

3 ⅓ cups white bread flour, plus extra for dusting • 1 tbsp. instant yeast • 2 tsp. salt • ⅓ cup sugar • 4 tbsp. lukewarm water • 5 eggs • 2 sticks plus 1 tbsp unsalted butter, softened, plus extra for the pans • 2 egg yolks • 2 tbsp. milk

MAKES 2 brioche

This is another soft dough, similar to panettone dough, and is best made using a mixer. You need to start making this the day before you intend to bake it.

1. Mix the flour, yeast, salt, sugar, water, and whole eggs using the paddle attachment of a mixer. Add the butter, one-third at a time, then increase speed to medium. Mix until the dough is elastic, 15 minutes. Transfer to a large, clean bowl, cover, and chill overnight.

2. Divide dough in two. Using floured hands, shape each piece into a ball, cover and set aside, 20 minutes.

3. Brush two fluted brioche pans liberally with butter and dust with a little flour. Put aside.

4. For each brioche, divide each ball in two, one about a quarter of the dough. Follow steps **a**, **b** and **c** (see right).

5. Cover and leave to rise in a warm place until doubled in size, 1–2 hours.

6. Preheat the oven to 400° F. For the glaze, beat the egg yolks with the milk and brush over the brioches. Transfer to the oven and bake 10–15 minutes, then reduce the oven temperature to 350° F. Continue baking until risen and golden brown, 35–40 minutes. Allow to cool before serving in slices.

step a Shape the larger piece into a ball, then make a hole in the center, pushing down with your finger until you break through the bottom.

step b Shape the second piece into a tapered cylinder. Cut through the tapered end halfway up. Put the cut end in the hole in the larger ball, pulling it through and tucking under the base. Drop into prepared tin.

step c Tuck the top edge of the large piece into the hole around the smaller piece—this will help keep the two pieces together as they rise. Repeat to make the second brioche.

Bread and butter pudding

6 tbsp. unsalted butter, softened, plus extra for greasing • 1 cup milk • 1 cup heavy cream • 1 vanilla pod, split • about 6 slices from day-old white loaf, crusts removed • 2 tbsp. apricot jelly • 2 tbsp. dried apricots, chopped • 1 tbsp. raisins • 2 tbsp. golden raisins • 6 egg yolks • 4 tbsp. sugar • light cream for serving

SERVES 8

This is a decadently rich dessert. Save it for special occasions and serve in small quantities. The better the quality of the bread, the better the pudding will taste.

1. Preheat the oven to 350° F. Lightly butter a shallow 5-cup ovenproof dish.

2. Put the milk, cream, and vanilla pod into a saucepan and heat gently just to simmering point. Remove from the heat and allow to infuse, 15 minutes.

3. Butter the bread generously. Spread half the slices with the apricot jelly. Cut all the bread slices diagonally into four triangles and use the bread spread with jelly to line the bottom of the dish. Scatter the apricots, raisins, and golden raisins over the bread in the dish. Arrange the remaining bread triangles attractively on top.

4. Meanwhile, whisk the egg yolks and sugar together until pale and creamy. Strain the milk and cream mixture onto the egg yolks and sugar, whisking all the time. Carefully pour the custard mixture over the bread as evenly as possible. Press the bread gently into the custard. Set aside, 20–30 minutes.

5. Transfer the dish to the oven and bake until the custard is just set and the bread is golden and crisp on top, 30–35 minutes. Serve warm with cream.

For recipe illustration, see page 14.

Plaited fruit loaf

generous 1 cup mixed candied and dried fruit, e.g., pineapple, raisins, golden raisins, orange peel, glacé cherries, roughly chopped • 4 tbsp. rum • 1 ½ cups white bread flour • ¼ tsp. salt • 1 ½ tsp. instant yeast • 2 tbsp. golden brown sugar • ½ cup lukewarm milk • 1 egg, beaten • ¼ cup almond paste, shredded • 6 tbsp. apricot jelly • 1 tbsp. unsalted butter • 1 tbsp. sugar • 1 tbsp. honey

SERVES 6–8

This is an unusual and beautiful loaf. Vary the fruit and alcohol according to taste—substitute all vine fruits, for example, or use brandy instead of rum.

1. Put the fruit in a bowl and add the rum. Cover and soak overnight.

2. Mix the flour, salt, yeast, and sugar. Make a well in the center and add the milk and egg. Mix to a soft dough. Knead until smooth, 10 minutes. Shape into a ball and put into a clean bowl. Cover and leave to rise, 1 hour, until doubled.

3. Meanwhile, mix the soaked fruit, almond paste, and jelly together. Preheat the oven to 400° F. Knead the dough again briefly for about 1 minute, then on a lightly floured surface, roll out to a 12- x 14-inch rectangle. Trim to a neat shape.

4. Spread the filling in a 3-inch strip down the center of the rectangle leaving a margin of 2 inches at each end. Make diagonal cuts, each about ¾-inch wide in the dough down either side of the filling.

5. Fold the strips of dough up over the filling, overlapping alternate strips. Tuck in the two ends. Transfer to a greased baking sheet.

6. Cover with oiled plastic wrap and leave to rise, 20 minutes. Melt the butter, sugar, and honey and brush over the dough. Transfer to the oven and bake until golden, 20–25 minutes. Let cool then slice.

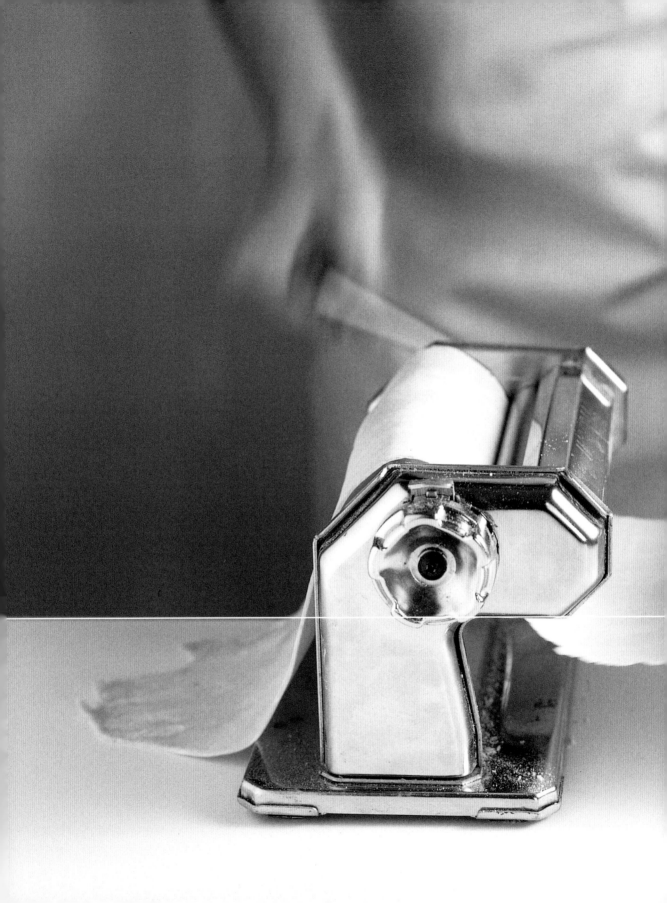

pasta

pasta introduction

Although a huge range of fresh pasta is readily available, often the commercially prepared variety is inferior to good quality dried pasta. Homemade fresh pasta however, using the best quality ingredients, is unbeatable.

mixing the dough

Fresh pasta is not very difficult to make, being only a combination of flour, eggs, and salt. The most difficult part of the process is getting the texture right so that it is neither sticky nor too dry and crumbly. As with pastry, this is best achieved through practice. The perfect pasta dough feels a little like very soft leather and is cool to the touch. When mixing the dough, add any water only a drop at a time and only if absolutely necessary to bring the dough together. Knead the dough, following the instructions in the recipe, until it is smooth. Fortunately, the dough gets extra kneading when it is passed through the pasta machine, so after the dough has rested you can let the machine do the work for you. A pasta machine, though not essential, is a worthwhile investment if you make pasta often. It is very difficult to roll the pasta dough thinly enough without one. Once the dough is rolled out, you should be able to see your hand through it. This is easily achieved with a machine, but is a lot of hard work with a rolling pin.

how long will it keep?

Pasta dough is best made and used on the same day because if left overnight in the fridge, the flour will begin to oxidize, giving the dough dark specks which although not harmful, are unappetizing. However, fresh pasta dough can be frozen successfully for up to two months if wrapped well or in an airtight container. It is also possible to make the dough, cut it into the required shape, then leave it to dry. Pasta left to dry this way can then be kept in an airtight container in the fridge for several days.

If you should find yourself with any leftover cooked pasta, keep it well covered in the fridge, either with or without sauce. The best way to reheat pasta without any loss of texture is in the microwave.

how long does it take to cook?

All pasta, whether fresh or dried, should be cooked until al dente—which means literally "to the tooth"— or until still firm to the bite and not soft but without a hard uncooked center. The time this takes will vary depending on the type of pasta, the shape, and the thickness. The most important thing is that the pasta should be added to a large amount of salted water which has come to a rolling boil. Stir the pasta once or twice during cooking, though if it's in a big pot with plenty of water, it won't stick. There is no need to add oil to the water if you cook pasta this way.

Pasta the basic method

The best flour to use for making pasta is 00 italian pasta flour, readily available from Italian delis, as well as many large supermarkets. Alternatively, substitute half all-purpose flour and half white bread flour. See the recipe on page 71 for ingredients to prepare the basic pasta dough.

A pasta machine is a worthwhile investment if you plan to make a lot of fresh pasta. Rolling dough by hand takes a lot of hard work to get it thin enough. A hand-cranked pasta machine will do the job very well and will last for many years.

 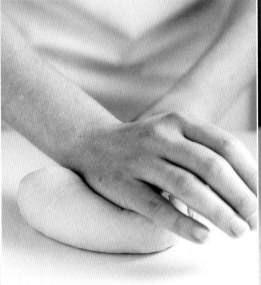 

step 1 Sift the flour and salt together into a bowl. Turn onto a clean surface and make a well in the center. Add the eggs, egg yolk, and oil. Gradually work these into the flour, adding a little extra water if necessary to make a smooth dough that is not sticky.

step 2 Turn the dough onto a lightly floured surface and knead until the dough is smooth and soft, 6–8 minutes. It should feel like soft leather. Form the dough into a neat ball and wrap in plastic wrap. Chill for at least 30 minutes before rolling.

step 3 Unwrap the dough and divide into eight equal pieces. Cover all but one of the pieces with plastic wrap until needed. Flatten one piece so that it will pass through the pasta machine rollers. With the machine at its widest setting, pass the dough through.

step 4 Fold the dough in three, rotate the dough a quarter turn, and pass through the machine again. Continue to pass the pasta sheet through the machine rollers, narrowing the gap by one setting each time, dusting with a little semolina flour if it begins to feel at all sticky.

step 5 If you are making noodles, it is best to stop at the second-to-last setting. For making filled pasta, or if you need to use the sheets to make lasagna, carry on to the last, and finest, setting. For noodles, the dough sheets should be hung over a pasta hanger, or draped over a clean wooden pole for about 5 minutes to dry slightly. If filling the pasta, it can be used straightaway, while still moist.

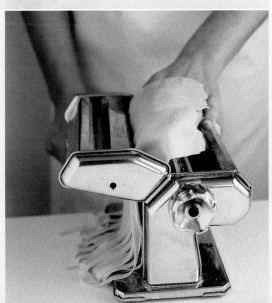

step 6 Fit the pasta cutter to the machine and pass each sheet of dough through the required cutters. Hang the noodles, again using a pasta hanger or drape over a pole until all the pasta is cut. Leave until dry but not stiff then coil the noodles into nests. Leave on a generously floured dishtowel or in an airtight container until needed.

Basic pasta dough with fresh tomato sauce

1 ½ cups 00 flour • 1 tsp. salt • 2 medium eggs plus 1 egg yolk • 1 tbsp. extra-virgin
olive oil • semolina flour, for dusting
For the sauce • 3–4 anchovy fillet in oil, drained • 2 tbsp. milk • 2 tbsp olive oil • 2
garlic cloves, finely sliced • large pinch chilli flakes • 1 cup cherry tomatoes, halved
handful basil leaves, roughly torn • freshly grated Parmesan, to serve

SERVES 4

1. Follow steps 1–6 of the basic pasta method (see pages 68–69),
cutting the dough into tagliatelle.

2. Put the anchovy fillets into a small bowl and cover with the milk.
Leave to stand for about 10 minutes and drain, discarding the milk.
Chop the anchovies finely.

3. Heat the oil in a large frying pan and add the anchovies, garlic
and chill flakes. Cook for 3–4 minutes over a medium heat until the
anchovies have dissolved. Increase the heat and add the tomatoes.
Toss and cook, about 2 minutes. Add the basil leaves and cook
briefly.

4. Meanwhile, bring a large pot of salted water to a boil. Drop in
the noodles and cook until al dente, about 2–3 minutes. Drain well.
Toss the noodles with the tomato mixture. Season to taste and
serve with grated Parmesan.

Ravioli with tiger shrimp and roasted tomato sauce

1 lb. ripe tomatoes, peeled and quartered • 1 tsp. olive oil • ¼ cup unsalted butter, softened • 1 tbsp. lemon juice • 2 tbsp. chopped fresh basil • 1 lb. raw peeled tiger shrimp • 1 tbsp. chopped fresh parsley • 1 tbsp. chopped fresh chives • 1 tsp. grated lemon peel • 4 tbsp. heavy cream • 1 quantity lemon pasta dough (see page 86), prepared to the end of step 2 in the basic method (see page 68) • semolina for dusting • sprigs of basil and lemon quarters to garnish

SERVES 4

1. Preheat the oven to 425° F. Drizzle the tomato quarters with the olive oil and put into a roasting pan at the top of the oven. Roast until soft and a little charred, about 15–20 minutes.

2. Remove from the oven and put into a food processor along with the butter, lemon juice, and half the basil. Process until smooth. Pass the sauce through a sieve to remove the seeds and season to taste.

3. Very finely chop the shrimp and mix with the parsley, chives, remaining basil, lemon peel, and cream. Season well and set aside.

4. Continue to follow steps 3,4, and 5 of the basic pasta method (see pages 68–69),rolling the pasta for filling. You should have eight sheets.

5. Lay one sheet on a work surface, keeping the remaining sheets covered. Follow steps **a**, **b**, and **c** (see right). Generously dust a tray with semolina and lay the rounds on the tray. Sprinkle with more semolina. As the filling is very moist, do not leave for longer than 30 minutes.

6. Cook ravioli in a large pot of boiling salted water in batches until al dente, 2–3 minutes. Drain well and divide between serving dishes. Spoon over the sauce and garnish with sprigs of basil and lemon.

step a Dot teaspoons of the mixture at 2–3-inch intervals. Brush around the filling with a little water.

step b Take a second pasta sheet and carefully lay over the first sheet, pressing down around the filling to exclude any air pockets.

step c Using a 3-inch fluted biscuit cutter, cut around the filling.

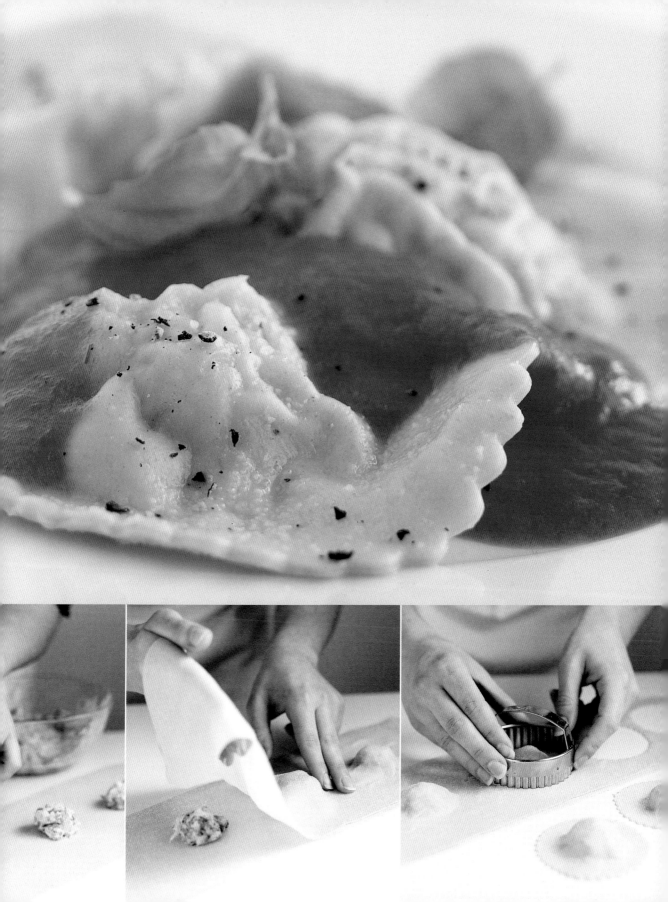

Ravioli with pumpkin and crispy prosciutto

1 lb. piece of pumpkin or butternut squash, seeds removed, and peeled • 3 tbsp. olive oil • ½ cup Provolone or Fontina cheese • 3 tbsp. freshly grated Parmesan • 1 tbsp. chopped fresh basil • 1 tbsp. chopped fresh parsley • 1 tbsp toasted pine nuts, roughly chopped • 1 egg yolk • 2 tbsp. heavy cream • 1 quantity basic pasta dough (see page 71), prepared to the end of step 2 • 4 slices prosciutto • 8 large sage leaves

SERVES 4

1. Preheat the oven to 375° F. Cut the pumpkin into large chunks and brush 2 tbsp. of oil over them. Bake until tender, about 30–40 minutes. Allow the pumpkin to cool slightly, then put the flesh into a large bowl and mash until smooth. Add the cheeses, basil, parsley, pine nuts, egg yolk, and cream. Season and set aside.

2. Follow steps 3–5 of the basic pasta method (see pages 68–69), rolling the pasta for filling. You should have eight sheets of pasta. Keep covered.

3. Lay one sheet of pasta onto a lightly floured surface. Dot teaspoonfuls of the filling at 2½-inch intervals. Brush the edges and between the stuffing with a little water. Carefully lay a second sheet of pasta over the top and press along the edges and between the stuffing to seal. Cut between the stuffing and trim the edges using a zigzag cutter to make little squares. Repeat using the remaining pasta and filling to make 20–24 ravioli.

4. Cook ravioli in a large pot of boiling salted water in batches until al dente, 3 minutes. Drain thoroughly and transfer to a serving dish. Fry prosciutto, one slice at a time, in the remaining oil in a skillet over a high heat until crisp, 30 seconds each side. Drain on paper towels. Reduce the heat and add the sage leaves. Cook gently until the leaves darken and turn crisp. Drain on paper towels. To serve, top the pasta with the crispy prosciutto and sage leaves. Drizzle with the oil from the pot. Serve with extra Parmesan.

Wide noodles with roasted wild mushrooms, garlic, and parsley

3 cups mixed wild mushrooms, cleaned and sliced • 4 tbsp. olive oil • 2 garlic cloves, sliced • ½ cup vegetable stock • ½ cup heavy cream • 2 tbsp. chopped fresh parsley • 3 tbsp. freshly grated Parmesan, plus extra to serve • 1 quantity chili-flavored pasta dough (see page 84)

SERVES 4

1. Preheat the oven to 400° F. Clean the mushrooms by brushing or wiping with a damp cloth. Chop or slice into large pieces. Leave smaller mushrooms whole. Put the mushrooms into a shallow roasting tray and drizzle with 2 tbsp. of the oil. Add the garlic and mix together. Transfer to the top of the oven and roast until the mushrooms are tender, but still firm.

2. Remove the mushrooms from the oven. Transfer to a large bowl. Put the roasting tray over a low flame and add the vegetable stock, stirring well to scrape up any sediment from cooking the mushrooms. Bring to a boil and reduce by half. Stir in the cream, parsley, and Parmesan. Add mushrooms and simmer briefly.

3. Follow the instructions for making chili pasta (see page 85) following the basic pasta method to the end of step 5 (see pages 68-69) and rolling the pasta for noodles. You should have eight sheets. Cut each sheet into long, wide noodles.

4. Cook the pasta in a pot of salted boiling water, 2–3 minutes. Drain well. Top the pasta with the sauce, and grated Parmesan.

Cappelletti stuffed with prosciutto, mozzarella, and sun-dried tomatoes

2 oz. prosciutto, finely chopped • 4 oz. buffalo mozzarella, drained and cut into fine dice • 2 oz. sun-dried tomatoes in oil, drained and finely chopped • ⅓ cup pitted black olives, finely chopped • 1 tbsp. each chopped fresh parsley and basil • 1 quantity of herb pasta dough (see page 86) • 4 tbsp. extra-virgin olive oil • freshly grated Parmesan, to serve

SERVES 4

The filling ingredients need to be very finely diced or they tend to break through the thin pasta.

1. Mix the prosciutto, mozzarella, tomatoes, olives, parsley and basil together. Season and set aside. Follow the instructions for making herb pasta using your preferred method (see page 86) and the basic pasta method to the end of step 5 (see pages 68–69), rolling the pasta for filling. You should have eight sheets.

2. Follow steps **a**, **b**, and **c** (see right). Repeat to make all the cappelletti, placing them on a clean floured dishtowel as you go.

3. Bring a large pot of salted water to a rolling boil and add the pasta, in batches if necessary. Cook until al dente, 2–3 minutes.

4. Toss the hot pasta with the olive oil, season with plenty of black pepper, and serve with freshly grated Parmesan.

step a Using a fluted 3-inch biscuit cutter, cut as many rounds from the pasta as you can. Cover and leave until slightly dry but still pliable.

step b Put a teaspoonful of the prosciutto mixture in the center of one circle. Brush all around with water, then fold over to enclose the filling and make a crescent shape. Press down all around to seal.

step c Hold the pasta shape with the fold pointing towards you and bring the two corners across to meet, pinching the ends together to seal, moistening with a little water if necessary.

Pappardelle with zucchini, sun-dried tomatoes, basil, and pine nuts

1 quantity basic pasta dough (see page 71) • 3 tbsp. extra-virgin olive oil • 1 tbsp. pine nuts • 2 garlic cloves, sliced • 2 medium zucchini, thinly sliced • large pinch chili flakes • 2 tsp. grated lemon peel • 4 sun-dried tomatoes, chopped • handful basil leaves, roughly torn • freshly grated Parmesan, to serve

SERVES 4

1. Follow steps 1–5 in the basic pasta method (pages 68–69), rolling the pasta for making noodles. Roll the pasta sheets from one narrow end into sausages. Using a sharp knife, cut the pasta crosswise into ⅓ inch wide strips. Hang the strips on a pasta hanger or drape over a clean pole until needed.

2. Heat 1 tbsp. of the oil in a large skillet or wok. Add the pine nuts and garlic and cook gently until golden. Remove with a slotted spoon and drain on paper towels. Set aside.

3. Add an additional 1 tbsp. of the oil and the zucchini. Increase the heat slightly and cook, stirring occasionally, until golden, about 5 minutes. Return the pine nuts and garlic to the pan with the lemon peel and sun-dried tomatoes. Cook until heated through, about 1 minute.

4. Meanwhile, bring a large pot of salted water to a rolling boil. Add the pasta and cook until al dente, 2–3 minutes. Drain, reserving a little of the water. Add the pasta to the pan with the zucchini along with the basil. Season well and mix together, adding a little of the reserved water if it seems a little dry. Divide between serving plates and top with freshly grated Parmesan. Serve immediately.

Mushroom tortelloni

¼ cup dried porcini or boletus mushrooms • generous ½ cup boiling water • ¼ cup pancetta or bacon, finely chopped • 1 tbsp. butter • 1 tbsp. olive oil • ½ lb. flat mushrooms, finely chopped • 1 garlic clove, minced • 2 tsp. grated lemon peel • ½ cup ricotta • 2 tbsp. freshly grated Parmesan, plus extra to serve • 1 small egg • 1 quantity basic pasta dough (see page 71) • 2 tbsp. butter, melted

SERVES 4

1. Put the dried mushrooms into a bowl and pour over the boiling water. Leave to soak, 20 minutes. Drain, reserving the soaking liquid. Finely chop the mushrooms.

2. Fry the pancetta in the butter and oil over a medium heat, 2–3 minutes. Add the chopped soaked mushrooms, flat mushrooms, and garlic. Cook over high heat, stirring, until the mushrooms have softened and released their liquid. Add the reserved soaking liquid, straining it if necessary to remove any grit. Simmer until all the liquid has evaporated and the mushrooms have started frying again.

3. Remove from the heat and add the lemon peel. Stir well and let cool. Stir in the ricotta, Parmesan, and egg. Season. Follow steps 1–5 of the basic pasta method (see pages 68–69), rolling the pasta for filling. You should have eight sheets of pasta. Cover.

4. Cut pasta into 3-inch squares. Put a teaspoon of filling in the middle. Brush around the filling and up to the edges then fold in half diagonally to form a triangle. Press down well to seal. Place your index finger against the folded edge and bring the two corners around it to meet, pinching the ends together to seal, moistening with a little water if necessary. Repeat to make all the tortelloni.

5. Cook tortelloni in a large pot of boiling salted water in batches until al dente, 2-3 minutes. Drain and toss with melted butter. Serve with some extra freshly grated Parmesan.

Two-toned ravioli with ricotta

1 tbsp. olive oil • 14-oz. can chopped tomatoes • 2 garlic cloves, minced • 1 tbsp. chopped fresh basil • pinch sugar • ½ quantity each plain and spinach pasta dough (see page 85) • extra flour, for dusting •1 cup fresh ricotta • 3 tbsp. finely chopped mixed fresh herbs, e.g., basil, chives, Italian parsley • 2 tsp. grated lemon peel • 1 tbsp. fresh lemon juice • 3 tbsp. freshly grated Parmesan, plus extra for serving • 1 egg, lightly beaten

SERVES 4

1. Put the oil, tomatoes, 1 minced garlic clove, basil, sugar, and seasoning into a medium saucepan. Bring to a boil and cover. Reduce the heat and simmer very gently, 30 minutes. Simmer, uncovered, until thickened, an additional 15 minutes.

2. For the filling, beat together the ricotta, herbs, lemon peel and juice, Parmesan, egg, and seasoning. Chill until needed.

3. Follow the instructions for making spinach pasta (see page 85) and plain pasta using the basic pasta method to the end of step 5 (see pages 68–69) rolling the pasta for filling. You should have four sheets of plain pasta and four sheets of spinach pasta. Lay one sheet of plain pasta on a work surface. Dot with the filling about every 3 inches. Brush around the filling with a little water. Take a sheet of spinach pasta and carefully lay over the first, pressing down around the filling to exclude any air pockets.

4. Using a sharp knife, trim the ends and long sides to leave an even margin around the filling. Cut between the filling to make squares. Set aside on a plate or baking tray dusted with semolina. Continue to make the remaining ravioli, between 20 and 24.

5. Bring a large pot of salted water to a rolling boil. Add the pasta, in batches if necessary and cook until al dente, 2–3 minutes. Drain.

6. Divide between serving plates and spoon the tomato sauce over. with extra freshly grated Parmesan.

Roast vegetable lasagna

1 large red bell pepper, deseeded and cut into chunks • 2 small zucchini, cut into chunks • 2 red onions, each cut into 8 wedges • 6 garlic cloves • 1 medium eggplant, cut into chunks • 2 tbsp. olive oil • 2 large sprigs fresh thyme • 2 fresh bay leaves • 2 x 11 oz. jars fresh tomato sauce • 10 oz. jar artichokes in oil, drained and halved if large • 2 oz. sun-dried tomatoes • 1 lb. 2 oz. ricotta • 2 eggs, beaten • 4 tbsp. freshly grated Parmesan, grated • ½ quantity basic pasta dough (see page 71), prepared to the end of step 5 in the basic pasta method for filling (see pages 68–69)   **SERVES 4**

1. Preheat the oven to 400° F. In a large bowl, toss the pepper, zucchini, onions, whole garlic cloves, and eggplant with the olive oil. Tip everything onto a shallow roasting tray or heavy baking sheet. Tuck the thyme sprigs and bay leaves in among the vegetables. Cook near the top of the oven, turning once or twice, until tender and golden at the edges, 40 minutes. Reduce the oven temperature to 375° F.

2. Remove the whole herbs. Mix the vegetables with the tomato sauce, artichokes, and sun-dried tomatoes. Set aside.

3. Reserving about 3 tablespoons of the Parmesan, in a large bowl, beat the ricotta until soft, then mix in the eggs, remaining Parmesan, and plenty of seasoning. Set aside.

4. Spread a large spoonful of the vegetable mixture over the bottom of an ovenproof dish measuring about 8 x 10 x 2½ inches. Trimming the sheets to fit, top with a layer of pasta. Now add half the remaining vegetable mixture and top with half the remaining pasta. Add the last of the vegetable mixture and the final layer of pasta and top with the ricotta mixture. Sprinkle with the reserved Parmesan.

5. Bake in the center of the oven until bubbling and golden, about 40–45 minutes.

Four-cheese sauce with spinach pasta

2 tbsp. butter • 8 sage leaves • ⅔ cup dolcelatte, crumbled • 1¼ cups mascarpone •
1 cup taleggio or fontina cheese, chopped • ¾ cup freshly grated Parmesan, plus extra
to serve • 1 quantity spinach pasta dough (see page 85)

SERVES 4

1. Follow the instructions for making spinach pasta (see page 85) following the basic pasta method to the end of step 6 (see pages 68–69), cutting the pasta into tagliatelle.

2. Melt the butter in a saucepan until foaming, then add the sage leaves. Cook gently until fragrant and the leaves are crisp, about 1 minute. Drain on paper towels and set aside.

3. Add the dolcelatte, mascarpone, and taleggio or fontina to the same pan and allow to melt slowly over a gentle heat.

4. Stir in the Parmesan until melted and season to taste. Be careful adding salt, as Parmesan, dolcelatte, and taleggio are all quite salty cheeses.

5. Meanwhile, bring a large pot of salted water to a rolling boil and add the pasta. Cook until al dente, 2–3 minutes. Drain well.

6. Put the pasta into a large serving bowl and toss with the sauce. Garnish with crispy sage leaves and serve immediately.

Flavored pasta

**Check out the basic pasta recipe on page 71, then
choose your favorite flavoring.**

Mushroom

Soak ½ cup of dried wild mushrooms in generous ½ cup boiling
water until softened, about 20 minutes. Drain well and squeeze
any excess liquid from the mushrooms. Chop very finely, using a
food processor if possible. Add to the basic pasta recipe along with
the eggs.

Chili

Deseed and very finely chop 1 or 2 hot red chilies. Add to the basic pasta recipe along with the eggs.

Spinach

Blanch 2 oz. fresh spinach until wilted. Refresh under cold water and drain well. Squeeze out any excess water, then chop very finely or purée in a food processor. Add to the basic pasta recipe with the eggs, reducing the water to 2 tsp., adding more only if necessary.

Sundried tomato

Beat the eggs with 2 tbsp. sundried tomato purée before adding to the flour in the basic pasta recipe.

Saffron

Soak a large pinch of saffron strands in 1 tbsp. of hot water until the water cools, about 20 minutes. Replace the whole egg in the basic pasta recipe with the saffron water.

Herb

There are two ways to make herb pasta.

Method 1. Add 3 tbsp. of very finely chopped mixed herbs to the flour and salt in the basic recipe.

Method 2. Make the basic pasta method up to the end of step 4 (see pages 68–69). Pass the pasta sheets through the rollers until you have changed the setting three times. Lay the sheet on a floured surface and lay whole soft herb leaves, e.g., basil, Italian parsley, cilantro, dill, thyme, or chives or a mixture, over half the dough to cover it. Fold over the other half to enclose and pass through the pasta machine again. Continue as in the main recipe. The herbs will stretch with the dough and create a speckled effect.

Black peppercorn

Coarsely crush 2 tsp. black peppercorns using a mortar and pestle or spice grinder. Stir into the flour along with the salt in the basic pasta recipe.

Lemon

Finely grate the peel from two lemons and stir into the flour along with the salt in the basic pasta recipe.

Olive

Beat the eggs with 2 tbsp. black olive paste or tapenade before adding to the flour in the basic pasta recipe.

Beet

Purée two cooked beets until very smooth, passing through a sieve if necessary. Leave out 1 egg from the basic pasta recipe.

Chocolate

Replace ⅓ cup of the flour in the basic recipe with an equal amount of sifted cocoa.

Squid ink

Add one sack of squid ink (available from fishmongers and large supermarkets) to the basic recipe, along with the whole eggs, leaving out the egg yolk.

Seared scallops in brown butter with saffron pasta

⅜ cup unsalted butter • 1 tbsp. olive oil • 12 scallops, cleaned • 2 tsp. grated lemon peel • 2 tbsp. fresh lemon juice • 1 tbsp. chopped fresh parsley • ½ quantity saffron pasta dough (see page 85), cut into tagliatelle • lemon quarters, to serve

SERVES 4 as an appetizer

1. Heat a third of the butter with the oil in a large, heavy nonstick skillet until foaming and very hot. Add the scallops in two batches and cook until golden, about 2 minutes on each side. Remove the scallops from the pan and set aside in a warmed dish.

2. Reduce the heat to medium and add the remaining butter to the skillet. Swirl around until melted. Cook until the butter has started to brown and smells nutty, about 1–2 minutes. Add the lemon peel and juice and remove from the heat. Stir in the parsley and season to taste.

3. Meanwhile, bring a large pot of salted water to a rolling boil. Add the pasta and cook until al dente, 2–3 minutes. Drain well.

4. Divide the pasta between serving plates. Top each serving with three scallops. Drizzle over the butter sauce and serve immediately, with lemon quarters.

Pasta in brodo

4 lbs. chicken • 1 carrot, cut into large chunks • 1 stick celery, cut into large chunks • 1 onion, halved • 2 whole peeled garlic cloves • 6 black peppercorns • 1 bay leaf • 1 large sprig thyme • ½ quantity basic pasta dough (see page 71), prepared to the end of step 5 (see pages 68–69) • handful fresh herbs leaves—basil, flat-leaf parsley, sage, mint, tarragon • 2 tbsp. chopped fresh parsley

SERVES 6

1. Put the chicken into a large saucepan or stockpot along with the carrot, celery, onion, garlic, peppercorns, bay leaf, and thyme. Cover with water and bring very slowly up to a boil. Skim the surface regularly to remove any scum that rises. cover and simmer very gently, 1½ hours. Remove from the heat and let cool.

2. Carefully remove the chicken from the stock. Remove the skin and discard. Remove the flesh and set aside. Discard the carcass.

3. Strain the stock and chill overnight, if possible. The next day, remove any fat that has solidified from the top of the stock and discard. Put the stock into a large pot and bring to a boil. Boil until reduced to about 6 cups.

4. Continue to follow the basic pasta method to the end of step 5 (see pages 68–69), rolling the pasta for the filling. You should have 4 sheets. Follow steps **a**, **b**, and **c** (see right).

5. Return the stock to a large saucepan and bring up to a boil. Taste and season. Add the chopped cooked chicken flesh. Return to a boil and add the pasta squares. Cook until al dente, 2–3 minutes. Stir in the parsley and season to taste. Serve immediately.

step a Lay a sheet of pasta on a surface. Dampen lightly with water. Put individual leaves or small sprigs of herbs at regular intervals all along its length.

step b Top with a second sheet of pasta and press down. Using a rolling pin, gently roll over the top of the pasta to seal it.

step c Using a zigzag cutter, trim the edges of the pasta and cut into squares, ensuring that the herbs are in the middle of the squares. Set aside on a floured tray until needed.

Arugula and hazelnut pesto

2½ cups arugula leaves • 1 garlic clove, chopped • ¼ cup roughly chopped toasted hazelnuts • 2 oz. piece Parmesan • 6 tbsp. extra-virgin olive oil • 1 tbsp. capers, chopped • 1 quantity basic pasta dough (see page 71), cut into noodles • freshly grated Parmesan, to serve

SERVES 4

1. Put the arugula, garlic, and hazelnuts into the bowl of a food processor and chop finely. Break or chop the Parmesan into smaller pieces and add these to the arugula mixture. Process again until the cheese is finely chopped but still recognizable.

2. Add 2 tbsp. of the oil and process again briefly to mix.

3. Scrape the mixture into a bowl and add the remaining oil, capers, and seasoning.

4. Meanwhile, bring a large pot of salted water to a rolling boil. Add the pasta and cook until al dente, 2–3 minutes. Drain well.

5. Return the pasta to the pot and add the pesto. Stir well until all the pasta is well coated. Serve with freshly grated Parmesan.

Fresh crab, chili, and garlic with fine noodles

4 tbsp. good quality extra-virgin olive oil • 2 garlic cloves, finely chopped • 1 red chili, deseeded and finely chopped • ¾ lb. freshly picked crab meat • 2 tsp. grated lemon peel • 2 tbsp. fresh lemon juice • 1 quantity basic pasta dough (see page 71), cut into fine noodles • 1½ cups chopped fresh parsley

SERVES 4

1. Heat 2 tbsp. of the oil over a low heat in a large skillet and add the garlic and chili. Cook briefly stirring, 2 minutes.

2. Add the crab meat and lemon peel and juice, tossing everything together until well mixed. Cook until the crab meat is heated through, about 1–2 minutes.

3. Meanwhile, bring a large pot of salted water to a rolling boil. Add the pasta and cook until al dente, 2–3 minutes. Drain well.

4. Add the drained pasta and remaining oil to the skillet with the crab and stir well to mix. Season to taste and serve immediately.

Herb tagliatelle with lemon chicken

2 large boned chicken breasts, skin on • 2 tbsp. flour, well seasoned • ¼ cup butter • 1 tbsp. olive oil • ½ quantity herb pasta dough (see page 86), cut into tagliatelle • 2 tsp. grated lemon peel • 2 tbsp. fresh lemon juice • 1 tbsp. drained capers, roughly chopped if large

SERVES 2

1. Wash and dry the chicken breasts. Put the seasoned flour onto a plate and coat both sides of each chicken breast. Shake to remove any excess flour. Set aside.

2. Melt half the butter with the oil in a skillet until foaming. Add the chicken breasts, skin side down, and cook over a low heat until deep golden, about 10 minutes.

3. Turn the chicken breasts and cook on the second side for an additional 10 minutes.

4. Turn the chicken breasts again and cook until the chicken is cooked through, an additional 5–10 minutes.

5. Meanwhile, bring a large pot of salted water to a rolling boil. Add the pasta and cook until al dente, 2–3 minutes. Drain well.

6. Remove the cooked chicken breasts from the pan. Add the remaining butter and cook until foaming and beginning to brown. Add the lemon peel and juice and the capers. Scrape up any bits from the bottom of the pan. Remove from the heat and season.

7. Slice the chicken breasts thickly on the diagonal. Divide the pasta between serving dishes and top with the sliced chicken. Drizzle with the lemon butter sauce and serve immediately.

Tagliolini with spicy meatballs

1 lb. boneless pork shoulder or turkey breast • ½ lb. pancetta or bacon, chopped • 2 garlic cloves, chopped • 1 tsp. salt • pinch ground cinnamon • pinch ground allspice • large pinch chili flakes • ½ cup fresh bread crumbs • 1 egg, lightly beaten • 4 tbsp. olive oil • 1 onion, finely chopped • 2 lbs. ripe tomatoes, skinned and roughly chopped • generous ½ cup red wine • 1 tsp. dried oregano • 2 tbsp. chopped fresh basil • pinch of sugar • 1 quantity black peppercorn pasta dough (see page 86), cut into fine noodles • extra basil, to garnish • freshly grated Parmesan, to serve

SERVES 4

1. Cut the pork or turkey into chunks and put into the bowl of a food processor. Add the pancetta or bacon, garlic, salt, cinnamon, allspice, chili flakes, and freshly ground black pepper. Process until finely chopped. Transfer to a bowl, add the bread crumbs and egg, and mix thoroughly. Using wet hands, shape tablespoonfuls of the mixture into even-sized balls. Chill for at least 30 minutes.

2. Meanwhile, heat 2 tbsp. of the olive oil, then add the onion and fry until softened, 5 minutes. Add the tomatoes, red wine, oregano, half the basil, and the sugar and bring to a boil. Cover and simmer gently, 30 minutes.

3. Heat the remaining olive oil in a skillet over a medium heat. Add the meatballs in batches and cook, turning often, until golden, 5 minutes. As they brown, add them to the tomato sauce. Return the sauce to a boil and simmer until the meatballs are cooked and the sauce is thickened, 20–30 minutes. Stir in the remaining basil.

4. Meanwhile, bring a large pot of salted water to a rolling boil. Add the pasta and cook until al dente, 2–3 minutes. Drain well.

5. Divide the pasta between serving dishes and top with the meatball sauce. Garnish with more basil and serve with Parmesan.

Tomato pasta with Italian sausage and lentils

1 cup Puy or Umbrian lentils • 3 tbsp. olive oil • 1 onion, finely chopped • 1 lb. 2 oz. spicy Italian sausage • 2 garlic cloves, minced • 14-oz. can chopped tomatoes • 1¼ cups chicken broth or vegetable stock • 1 quantity sundried tomato pasta dough (see page 84), cut into wide noodles • 1 tbsp. chopped fresh parsley   **SERVES 4**

1. Pick over the lentils, looking for any grit. Rinse under running water and drain well.

2. Heat the oil in a large deep saucepan and add the onion. Cook over a low heat until soft and starting to brown, 5–7 minutes. Add the sausages and garlic, and cook until the sausages start to brown, 3–4 minutes. Add the drained lentils and continue cooking for an additional 1 minute.

3. Add the tomatoes and broth. Season lightly and bring to a boil. Cover, lower the heat, and simmer gently until the sausages and lentils are tender, 40–45 minutes. Check seasoning.

4. Meanwhile, bring a large pot of salted water to a rolling boil. Add the pasta and cook until al dente, 2–3 minutes. Drain well.

5. Divide the pasta between serving dishes and spoon over the sausages and lentils. Sprinkle with the chopped parsley and serve.

Ragù bolognese

2 tbsp. olive oil • 1 onion, finely chopped • 1 carrot, finely chopped • 1 stick celery, finely chopped • ½ cup bacon or pancetta, finely diced • 1¾ cups ground pork • 1¾ cups ground beef • 1¼ cups red wine • 2 tbsp. tomato paste • 1¼ cups beef broth • 4 tbsp. heavy cream • 1 quantity basic pasta dough (see page 71), cut into fine noodles • 1 tbsp. chopped fresh parsley

SERVES 4

1. Heat the oil in a large saucepan. Add the onion, carrot, and celery and cook gently for 10–12 minutes until softened.

2. Add the pancetta or bacon and cook for an additional 3–4 minutes before adding the pork and beef. Increase the heat and cook until the meat is no longer pink, about 8–10 minutes. You may want to drain off any excess fat at this stage.

3. Add the wine and simmer until nearly evaporated, about 10 minutes. Add the tomato paste and about half the beef broth. Bring to a boil and reduce the heat to a simmer.

4. Simmer gently about 1½ hours, adding more stock as necessary. Most of it will evaporate.

5. Bring a large pot of salted water to a rolling boil and add the pasta. Cook until al dente, about 1–2 minutes. Drain well.

6. Add the cream to the meat sauce and stir well. Simmer an additional 1 minute before adding the parsley. Season to taste. Toss the sauce with the drained pasta and serve immediately.

Pasta calabrese

6 tbsp. olive oil • ½ cup fresh white bread crumbs • 1 lb. broccoli florets • 3 anchovy fillets in oil (optional), drained and chopped • 2 garlic cloves, finely sliced • large pinch chili flakes • 2 tsp. grated lemon peel • 1 quantity of basic pasta dough (see page 71), cut into tagliatelle • freshly grated Parmesan, to serve

SERVES 4

1. Heat 2 tbsp. of the olive oil in a large skillet and add the bread crumbs. Cook, stirring often, until golden. Drain on paper towels.

2. Bring a large pot of salted water to a rolling boil and add the broccoli florets. Blanch for 3 minutes, then remove with a slotted spoon to a colander. Reserve the cooking water to boil the pasta. Refresh the broccoli under cold running water and drain again. Dry on paper towels.

3. Heat an additional 2 tbsp. of the oil in a large skillet or wok. Add the anchovy fillets, garlic, and chili flakes and cook over a medium heat until the anchovies have broken down and the garlic is starting to color, 2 minutes.

4. Add the broccoli florets and cook, stirring often, until the broccoli is heated through, about 4 minutes.

5. Meanwhile, return the pot of water in which you blanched the broccoli to a rolling boil. Add the pasta and cook until al dente, 2–3 minutes. Drain well.

6. Add the lemon peel, and remaining olive oil to the broccoli mixture and season well. Add the pasta to the pot and stir well to mix. Serve immediately, sprinkled with the bread crumbs and plenty of freshly grated Parmesan.

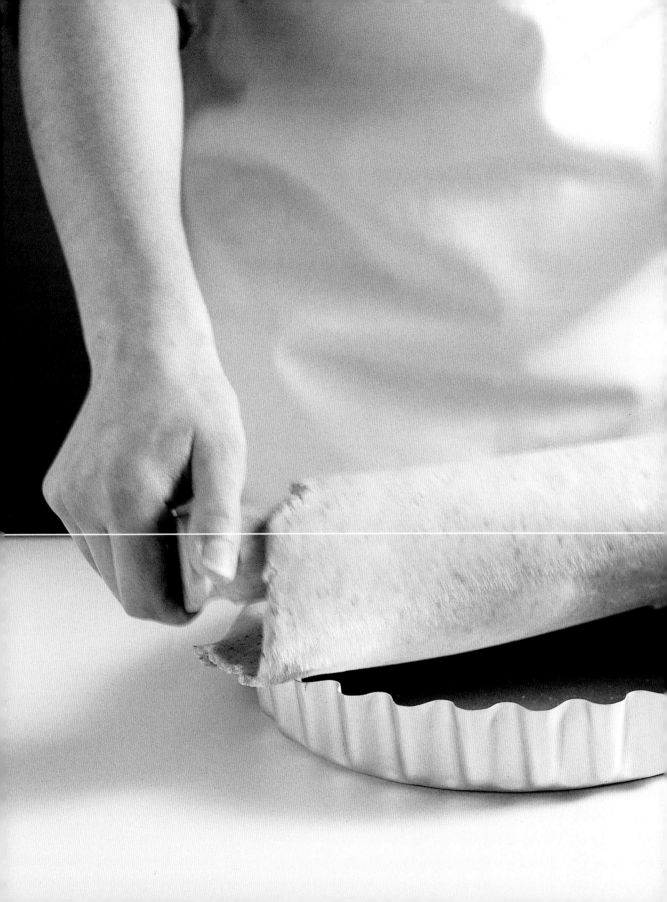

pastry

pastry introduction

pastry introduction Successful pastry-making relies on a light touch, careful handling, and accurate measuring. The golden rule is to keep everything cool—the dough, the work surface, any utensils, and your hands. All the recipes for pastry are made with butter as it gives the best flavor and crispest texture. The texture of the flour, however, will also determine the crispness of the finished pastry. If you like whole-wheat pastry, substitute half the all-purpose flour with whole-wheat flour, as using it alone can produce a very soggy result.

Another important element in the making of pastry is water. Too much and the pastry will be tough and will shrink back excessively in the pan. Too little and the dough will be difficult to handle and will fall apart easily when cooked. The only real way to judge the amount of water needed is to practice and get a feel for it. Although some kneading is required when making all the pastries, the idea is to bring the dough together so that it is smooth, but without the gluten "setting up," and keeping the butter in little pieces as they are rubbed in. This is what makes the pastry flaky—if overworked, it will end up tough and greasy.

Make shortcrust pastry either by hand or in a food processor. If you have naturally warm hands, opt for the food processor method. The butter can also be cut into the flour using two knives, but this is more time-consuming. The recipe for rough puff is very easy and makes a fabulously light, flaky pastry. If

you are worried about making puff pastry, or haven't the time, try this method instead. Puff pastry is, without question, the most difficult and time-consuming type of pastry to master and it does take some practice. But all-butter puff pastry is difficult to buy, so if full-flavor is what you're after, this is the pastry to make.

Baking blind

Once shortcrust pastry has been rolled and used to line a pan, it is often pre-cooked or "baked blind" before being filled. The reason for this is to ensure that the pastry base is cooked through and to stop the filling from soaking through. After lining the pan, put it into the fridge to rest, about 20–30 minutes. Alternatively, put in the freezer where it can stay for up to one month. You can bake blind from frozen. Remove the lined pan from the fridge or freezer and line with foil or waxed paper. Now add either specially made ceramic baking beans or use dried pulses or rice. The ceramic baking beans conduct the heat and help to cook the pastry as well as keeping it from puffing up in the oven. If you use dried pulses or rice, let them cool, then keep in a sealed jar especially for this purpose.

Shortcrust pastry the basic method A great deal

of mystique surrounds the making of shortcrust pastry. In fact, the method is very straightforward and just takes a little practice. If you're worried that your hands are too warm to rub the butter in as described below, try using that wire-ringed implement, a pastry blender, to cut the butter into small pieces. Alternatively, two knives work just as well. It's important to rest the dough before rolling or it may shrink upon cooking, producing an uneven result. See recipe on page 109 for ingredients to prepare the basic shortcrust pastry dough.

step 1 Sift the flour into a mixing bowl with the salt. Add the butter and using your fingertips, rub or cut the butter into the flour until the mixture resembles coarse bread crumbs.

step 2 Add 2 tbsp. of the water and using your hands, start to bring the dough together, adding a little more water if necessary. Do not use too much water or the resulting pastry will be tough.

step 3 Turn the dough onto a lightly floured surface and knead briefly, just until the dough is smooth. Form into a neat ball, flatten into a disk, and wrap in plastic wrap. Chill at least 30 minutes.

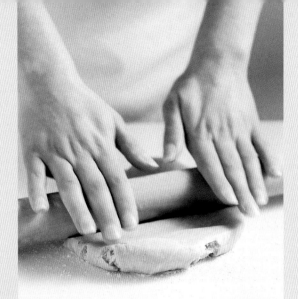

step 4 Remove the pastry from the fridge. Unwrap and put onto a lightly floured surface. Lightly flour the top of the dough and a rolling pin. Begin rolling the dough by exerting pressure on the rolling pin while rolling it back and forth. Try not to stretch the dough by pulling—allow the weight and pressure of the pin to roll the dough.

step 5 Roll the pastry into a rough circle at least 2 inches in diameter, larger than a loose-bottomed 9-inch fluted pastry ring. Gently roll the pastry onto the rolling pin, then unroll it over the ring to cover. Carefully press the pastry into the edge of the ring, removing any overhanging pastry with a knife.

step 6 Prick the base all over with a fork, being careful not to make holes right through the dough. This helps to keep the dough from rising in the middle during blind baking. Chill for 20 minutes.

Honey and mixed nut tart

generous 1 ¼ cups all-purpose flour • pinch salt • ⅜ cup cold butter, diced •
2–3 tbsp. cold water
For the filling • ⅜ cup butter • 1 cup honey • heavy cream, to serve • 2 ⅓ cups
mixed nuts, e.g., pecans, walnuts, hazelnuts, almonds

SERVES 8

Shortcrust pastry is really versatile. Here it encases a delicious honey and nut filling.

1. Follow the basic shortcrust pastry method (see pages 106–7) to the end of step 6.

2. Preheat the oven to 400° F. Remove the ring from the fridge and line with foil or waxed paper. Fill with baking beans and transfer to the oven. Bake 12 minutes then carefully remove the paper and beans. Return the pastry to the oven until pale golden, an additional 10 minutes. Cool on a wire rack.

3. Reduce the oven temperature to 375° F.

4. For the filling, put the butter and honey into a medium saucepan over a low heat. When the butter and honey have both melted together, increase the heat and allow to bubble until starting to darken, 1–2 minutes. Stir in the nuts and return the mixture to simmering point. Remove from the heat and allow to cool slightly.

5. Transfer the mixture to the prepared pastry shell. Return to the oven and bake until the nuts are golden and fragrant and the pastry is nicely browned, 5–7 minutes. Serve warm with cream.

Rough puff pastry the basic method

This is an unusual method for making rough puff pastry, as the dough includes baking powder and is bound with buttermilk. This helps to give the pastry a good rise as well as an excellent flavor. It produces a dough that is softer than butter puff pastry and so is best suited for savory rather than sweet recipes. This dough can be frozen, well-wrapped, for up to 2 months. Thaw completely before using. See the recipe on page 112 for ingredients to prepare the basic rough puff pastry dough.

1. Sift the flour, salt, baking powder, and baking soda into a mixing bowl. Cut the butter into dice, add to the flour, and rub together, using your fingertips until the mixture resembles very coarse bread crumbs. The pieces of butter should still be discernible, but all coated in flour.

2. Follow steps **a**, **b**, and **c** (see right).

3. Transfer the dough to a baking sheet or tray lined with waxed paper. Cover with plastic wrap and chill, about 20 minutes.

4. Remove from the fridge and repeat the rolling and folding twice more. Prepare to this point if using to top a pie or for use in the recipe that follows.

step a Stir in about half the buttermilk and begin mixing the dough together, adding just enough of the remaining buttermilk to make a soft dough.

step b Turn the dough onto a floured surface and dust with flour as well. Roll the dough out to ¾-inch thick. Lift the dough from the surface and fold it, like a letter, in thirds.

step c Give the dough a quarter turn. Flour the surface and dough again and reroll the dough into a rectangle of the same thickness. Repeat the folding and turning.

Butter biscuits

1 ½ cups all-purpose flour • ½ tsp. salt • 1 tsp. baking powder • pinch baking soda
¾ cup cold unsalted butter • 6 tbsp. cold buttermilk • 1 tbsp. melted butter, for
brushing
                                                    MAKES 10-12 biscuits

Although this recipe for rough puff pastry is ideal for topping savory meat pies, it also makes fabulous biscuits. The dough can be made ahead and refrigerated or frozen and then baked fresh to eat with soup, for breakfast, or with roast meat and gravy.

1. To make the rough puff pastry, follow the method on pages 110–11 up to the end of step 4.

2. Roll a final time to a ¾-inch thick rectangle. Now either cut the dough into triangles or use a biscuit cutter to cut the dough into rounds.

3. Put the cut dough about 1 inch apart on a paper-lined baking sheet. Cover with plastic wrap and chill, at least 20 minutes.

4. Preheat the oven to 475° F. Brush the tops of the biscuits with melted butter. Transfer the baking sheet to the oven and reduce the temperature to 375° F.

5. Bake until golden all over, 12–15 minutes. Let cool 5 minutes, then eat while still warm.

Puff pastry the basic method

Well-made, all butter puff pastry is a real indulgence. Making your own is time-consuming, but well worth the effort. This recipe makes about 1½ pounds. This dough freezes beautifully, however, so while some of the recipes only require half the recipe, the remaining half can be set aside and used for a quick recipe on another day. See the recipe on page 116 for ingredients to prepare the basic puff pastry dough.

1. Put one quarter of the flour into a bowl with the butter. Using an electric mixer, combine the butter and flour thoroughly. Scrape the butter paste onto a sheet of plastic wrap, shape into a 5- x 6-inch rectangle, and leave in a cool place (but not the fridge).

2. Put the remaining flour, egg yolks, water, and salt into a bowl and mix to a dough. If necessary, add a little more water, but the dough will soften on resting. Turn the dough onto a floured surface and knead until very smooth and elastic, about 10 minutes. Alternatively, put all the ingredients into the bowl of an electric mixer fitted with a dough hook and mix to a dough. Knead on a low speed, between 6–8 minutes.

3. Form the dough into a neat ball and wrap in plastic wrap. Rest in the fridge for at least 1 hour or overnight if possible.

4. Follow steps **a**, **b,** and **c** (see right).

5. Place on a plastic wrap-lined tray and cover with more plastic wrap. Chill for 1 hour.

6. Put the dough on a floured surface so the fold is to one side. Roll again as before and give the dough a single turn (see step **c**, right), followed immediately by another. Wrap in plastic wrap and chill overnight before using.

step a Lightly flour a work surface and roll out the dough to an 11-inch square. Place the rectangle of butter paste in the center and fold the corners of the dough over to completely enclose. Wrap in plastic wrap and chill, 30 minutes.

step b Place the dough on a lightly floured surface. Roll the dough out into a 16- x 28-inch rectangle. Fold one end in by a sixth, then the other end in by a sixth. Fold both ends until they meet in the center. Now fold the two together as if closing a book.

step c Turn the dough so that the fold is to one side. Roll dough as before and fold one end in by a third, repeat at the other end to cover the first fold. Fold in half from left to right again as if closing a book. Brush off excess flour. This step is a single turn.

Tomato and basil tartlets

2 ⅓ cups all-purpose flour • ¾ cup unsalted butter, softened •
2 egg yolks • 6 tbsp. cold water • 1 tsp. salt
For the tart filling • 24-28 ripe cherry or baby plum tomatoes,
halved • 1 tsp. finely chopped fresh rosemary or thyme • 6 tbsp.
extra-virgin olive oil • handful basil leaves, roughly torn

MAKES 8

**You will end up with about 1½ pounds of puff pastry and
you need only half to make 8 of these delightful tartlets.
Freeze the remaining pastry, well-wrapped, for use in
another recipe.**

1. To make the puff pastry, follow the basic method on pages
114–5, up to the end of step 6.

2. Next day, preheat the oven to 400° F. Roll out half the pastry to
a 8- x 17-inch rectangle and using a plain 4-inch biscuit cutter, cut
out eight rounds. Put onto a lightly greased baking sheet.

3. Divide the tomatoes between the rounds, leaving a ½-inch
border. Sprinkle with the rosemary and drizzle with 2 tbsp. of the
olive oil. Season well and bake until the pastry is risen and golden,
12–15 minutes. Meanwhile, put remaining oil and basil in a blender
or small food processor and blend until smooth. When the tartlets
are cooked, drizzle with the basil mixture and garnish with roughly
torn basil leaves. Serve hot.

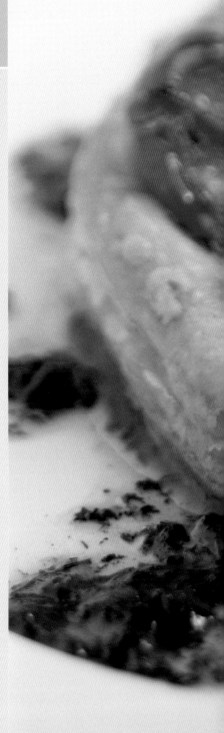

Chicken and spring vegetable pie

3 lbs. chicken • 1 large carrot, cut into chunks • 1 onion, halved • 1 celery stick, cut into chunks • 1 bay leaf • 1 sprig thyme • 6 black peppercorns • 1 lb. mixed spring vegetables, e.g., baby carrots, peas, asparagus, haricots verts, baby leeks, small zucchini or pattypan squashes, baby fennel • ¼ cup butter • 2 tsp. fresh thyme leaves • ¼ cup all-purpose flour • generous ½ cup heavy cream • 1 quantity rough puff pastry (see pages 114), prepared to the end of step 4 • 1 egg, beaten

SERVES 4-6

1. Gently simmer the chicken with carrot, onion, celery, bay leaf, thyme, peppercorns, and water to cover, in a covered pan, 1 hour. Skim off scum from the surface. Leave to go cold in pan. Carefully remove the chicken from the stock and set aside. Strain the stock into a clean saucepan and return to a boil. Simmer rapidly until reduced to 3¾ cups. Season. Skin chicken and cut flesh into chunks.

2. Scrub, trim, and slice until all the spring vegetables are the same size. Drop them into the boiling stock and return to the boil. Blanch for 3 minutes until tender. Remove with a slotted spoon and set aside, reserving the stock. Melt the butter in a pan, add the thyme and flour and stir well. Gradually add the reserved stock, stirring well after each addition, until smooth. Increase the heat, bring to a boil, stirring constantly, and simmer gently, 2 minutes. Remove from the heat and stir in the cream, reserved chicken, vegetables, and parsley. Season to taste.

3. Preheat the oven to 400° F. Roll out the prepared pastry and cut a strip just larger than the rim of your pie dish. Brush the rim of the dish with water and attach the strip. Cut another piece to make the lid. Spoon the filling into the pie dish. Dampen the pastry strip, add a pastry funnel, then top with the pastry lid. Crimp the edges to seal, or make a decorative edge. Use any pastry trimmings to decorate the top of the pie, then brush with beaten egg. Transfer to the center of the oven and bake until the pastry is risen and golden and the filling is bubbling, 25–30 minutes. Cool slightly before serving.

Potato, bacon, and egg pie

¾ cup butter, diced • 2 cups all-purpose flour • pinch salt • 1 tsp. fresh thyme leaves •
1 tsp. cumin seeds • 1 egg yolk • 1–2 tbsp. cold water • 1 lb. potatoes, diced • 1 tbsp.
olive oil • 1 onion, finely chopped • ½ lb. bacon, chopped • 2 tbsp. chopped fresh
parsley • 5 eggs

SERVES 4

1. For the pastry, rub the butter into the flour with the salt until the mixture resembles coarse bread crumbs. Stir in thyme and cumin.

2. Mix the egg yolk and 1 tbsp. of the water together and add to flour mixture. Start to bring the dough together, adding a little more water if necessary. Follow step 3 of the basic shortcrust pastry method (see pages 106–7).

3. Meanwhile, cook the potatoes in boiling salted water until just tender, 5 minutes. Drain well and set aside. Heat the oil in a skillet and add the onion. Cook over a medium heat until softened and starting to brown, 5–7 minutes. Add the bacon and cook an additional 5 minutes until the onion is brown and the bacon is crisp. Leave to cool slightly. Preheat the oven to 400° F.

4. Follow step 4 in the shortcrust pastry method (see pages 106–7), rolling out two-thirds of the pastry to fit a 9-inch pie plate. Use the pastry to line the pie plate, saving the trimmings to decorate the pie. Spoon in the cooked potato, onion, and bacon mixture and sprinkle with the chopped parsley. Season.

5. Make four little wells in the potato mixture and break an egg into each one. Roll out the remaining pastry to just larger than the pie plate. Brush a little water onto the rim of the dish and top with the lid. Press down well to seal. Make a decorative edge, if desired, and decorate with trimmings. Beat the remaining egg and brush over the top of the pie. Bake until golden, 30 minutes. Serve in wedges.

Beef and caramelized onion pies

4 tbsp. vegetable oil • 2 large onions, sliced • 1 tsp. brown sugar • 1½ lbs. lean rump steak, cubed • 2 tbsp. all-purpose flour • 1 carrot, finely chopped • 2 garlic cloves, finely chopped • ½ lb. baby button or baby chestnut mushrooms • generous ½ cup beef broth • generous ½ cup dark beer • 1 tbsp. tomato paste • 1 tbsp. Worcestershire sauce • 1 tbsp. fresh thyme leaves • 1 bay leaf • ¾ lb. potatoes, cubed • ½ quantity puff pastry (see pages 114–15), prepared to the end of step 6 • 1 egg, beaten

SERVES 4

1. Heat half the oil in a large skillet. Add the onions and cook over a medium heat until lightly golden, 5–7 minutes. Add the sugar, stir well, and cook until caramelized, 4–5 minutes. Set aside.

2. Preheat the oven to 275° F. Toss the meat cubes in the flour, shaking off and reserving any excess. Heat the remaining oil over a medium heat in a large flameproof casserole and add the meat. Cook until browned all over, 5–7 minutes. Add the carrot, garlic, and mushrooms and cook until softened, further 3–4 minutes. Stir in the rest of the flour. Gradually add the broth and beer.

3. Add tomato paste, Worcestershire sauce, thyme, and bay leaf. Bring to a boil, cover and cook in oven, 1 hour. Add the potatoes, return to the oven and cook until tender, an additional 20 minutes. Increase oven temperature to 400° F. Spoon the steak mixture into four 1¼ cup individual ovenproof pie dishes. Top with the onions.

4. Roll the pastry out thinly and cut four ovals or rounds about 2 inches wider than the pie dishes. From these, trim a 1-inch wide strip. Wet the rims of the dishes and attach the pastry strips. Wet the pastry strips and attach the pastry lids. Seal and make a decorative edge. Decorate with trimmings.

5. Brush the pastry with beaten egg. Bake until the pastry is risen and golden, 25 minutes. Let cool slightly before serving.

Mushroom tart with walnut pastry

⅓ cup walnuts • 1 cup all-purpose flour • pinch salt • ⅜ cup butter, diced • 2–3 tbsp. cold water • 2 tbsp. butter • 1 tbsp. vegetable oil • 1 small onion, finely chopped • ¾ lb. mixed fresh wild or cultivated mushrooms • 2 garlic cloves, finely chopped • pinch freshly grated nutmeg • 2 egg yolks • 1 cup heavy cream • 1 tbsp. chopped fresh parsley

SERVES 6

1. Grind the walnuts in a food processor or spice grinder until fine, but not pasty—if you overgrind them, they will become very oily and sticky which will make the pastry very difficult to handle. Follow the basic shortcrust pastry method (see pages 106–7) to the end of step 6, adding the ground nuts to the rubbed in mixture. Preheat the oven to 400° F.

2. Line the pastry with foil or waxed paper and fill with baking beans. Transfer to the oven and bake for 12 minutes. Remove the baking beans and foil or waxed paper and cook for an additional 10 minutes until golden. Remove from the oven and set aside to cool. Reduce the oven temperature to 350° F.

3. Melt the butter and vegetable oil in a large skillet. Add the onion and cook until softened, about 5 minutes. Increase the heat and add the mushrooms. Cook until softened, an additional 4–5 minutes. Add the garlic, nutmeg, and seasoning. Stir briefly and remove from the heat.

4. Spoon the mushroom mixture evenly over the pastry case. Whisk the egg yolks, cream, parsley, and seasoning together. Pour evenly over the mushrooms. Bake until just set, 30–35 minutes. Let cool 15 minutes before serving.

Caponata and feta cheese tart

scant 1 ¼ cups all-purpose flour • pinch salt • ⅓ cup butter, diced • 2 tsp. finely chopped fresh rosemary • 2–3 tbsp. cold water • 3 tbsp. olive oil • 1 medium eggplant, cut into ½-inch cubes • 3 celery sticks, thinly sliced • 14-oz. can chopped tomatoes • 2 tbsp. capers, drained and rinsed • ⅔ cup pitted black olives • 2 tbsp. red wine vinegar • 1 tbsp. sugar • 1 egg yolk, beaten • 2 cups feta cheese, crumbled • 1 tbsp. fresh thyme leaves

SERVES 6

1. To make the pastry, follow steps 1–6 of the basic shortcrust pastry method (see pages 106–7) , stirring the rosemary into the rubbed in mixture. Preheat the oven to 400° F. Line the pastry case with foil or waxed paper and fill with baking beans. Transfer to the oven and bake for 12 minutes. Remove the baking beans and foil or waxed paper and cook for an additional 10 minutes until golden. Remove from the oven and set aside to cool. Reduce the oven temperature to 350° F.

2. Heat the olive oil in a large skillet over a medium heat and add the eggplant. Fry until golden but not overcooked, about 10 minutes. Remove the eggplant from the pan using a slotted spoon and drain on paper towels. Set aside.

3. Add the celery and tomatoes to the pan and simmer 10 minutes. Add the capers, olives, vinegar, sugar, and seasoning. Cook until fairly thick, an additional 5 minutes. Stir in the eggplant and cook for a further 5 minutes until tender, but still holding their shape.

4. Remove from the heat and let cool.

5. Fold the egg yolk and feta cheese into the eggplant mixture and spoon it into the prepared pastry case. Sprinkle with the thyme leaves. Bake until the filling is bubbling, 12–15 minutes. Serve hot or warm with a green salad.

Duck tart with shallot chutney

1 cup whole walnuts or pecans • 1½ cups all-purpose flour • ½ tsp. salt • ½ cup cold butter • 3–4 tbsp. cold water • ¾ lb. skinned duck breast, thinly sliced • 2 tbsp. olive oil • ½ cup wild rice • 3 scallions, finely chopped • 1 tbsp. chopped mixed thyme, marjoram, oregano • 4 tbsp. dry sherry • 3 eggs, beaten • ⅔ cup heavy cream

For the chutney • ½ lb. shallots, peeled and halved • pinch sugar • 1 garlic clove, finely chopped • 1 tbsp. chopped fresh thyme • 2 tbsp. balsamic vinegar • generous ½ cup red wine   **SERVES 4**

1. To make the pastry, grind the walnuts or pecans in a food processor or spice grinder until fine, but not pasty—if you overgrind them, they will become very oily and sticky which will make the pastry very difficult to handle. Follow the basic shortcrust method (see pages 106–7) to the end of step 6, adding the ground nuts to the rubbed in mixture. Preheat the oven to 400° F. Line the pastry case with foil or waxed paper and fill with baking beans. Transfer to the oven and bake for 12 minutes. Remove the baking beans and foil or waxed paper and cook for an additional 10 minutes until golden. Remove from the oven and set aside to cool. Reduce the oven temperature to 375° F.

2. Bring a large pot of water to a boil and add the wild rice. Lower the heat and simmer until the rice is split and tender, about 35–45 minutes. Drain and set aside.

3. Heat the oil in a large skillet and add the duck. Stir-fry until browned and nearly cooked through, 3–4 minutes. Add the scallions. Cook until softened, 1 minute. Add the herbs and wild rice and cook an additional 2 minutes. Add the dry sherry and simmer until reduced and syrupy. Remove from the heat and season well. Let cool slightly. Spread evenly over the pastry case.

4. Whisk eggs, cream, and seasoning. Pour over duck mixture then bake, 25 minutes. Leave to cool about 15 minutes before serving.

5. Meanwhile, to make the shallot chutney, heat the remaining olive oil in a medium saucepan and add the shallots. Cook over a low heat until softened, about 10 minutes. Add the pinch of sugar and stir well. Cover and cook very gently until the shallots are golden and tender, an additional 20 minutes.

6. Add the garlic and thyme and cook briefly before adding the balsamic vinegar. Swirl around the pan to deglaze, then reduce until syrupy. Add the wine and cook until reduced to about 2 tbsp., about 5 minutes. Remove from the heat, season, and let the mixture cool before serving with the tart.

Tarte à la moutarde

Scant 1 cup all-purpose flour • pinch salt • ⅓ cup butter, diced • 2–3 tbsp. cold water •
3 tbsp. Dijon mustard • 1 cup Gruyère cheese, shredded • 7 oz. can chopped tomatoes,
drained • 3 egg yolks • 1 cup heavy cream

SERVES 4

1. To make the pastry, follow the steps in the basic shortcrust
pastry method (see pages 106–7) to the end of step 6.

2. Preheat the oven to 400° F. Remove the pastry-lined ring from
the fridge and line with foil or waxed paper. Fill with baking beans
and transfer to the oven. Bake 12 minutes, then carefully remove
the paper or foil and beans. Return to the oven an additional 5
minutes. Remove from the oven and let cool. Reduce the oven
temperature to 325° F.

3. Spread the mustard evenly over the base of the pastry. Sprinkle
over the cheese, then spread the tomatoes over the cheese. Whisk
the egg yolks and cream together with some seasoning. Pour over
the cheese and tomatoes.

4. Transfer to the oven and bake until just set and the pastry is
golden, about 1 hour. Allow to cool slightly before serving with a
crisp green salad and some crusty bread.

Potato and goat cheese tart

generous **1 cup all-purpose flour** • **pinch salt** • **⅓ cup butter, diced** • **2–3 tbsp. cold water** • **2 large potatoes, sliced** • **2 tbsp. olive oil** • **3 leeks, thinly sliced** • **1 garlic clove, finely chopped** • **1 tbsp. fresh thyme leaves** • **2 tbsp. pine nuts, toasted** • **4 oz. firm goat cheese, sliced thinly** • **3 egg yolks** • **⅔ cup heavy cream**

SERVES 4

1. For the pastry, follow the basic shortcrust pastry method (see pages 106–7) to the end of step 6. Preheat the oven to 400° F. Line the pastry case with foil or waxed paper and fill with baking beans. Transfer to the oven and bake for 12 minutes. Remove the baking beans and foil and cook for an additional 10 minutes until golden. Remove from the oven and leave to cool. Reduce the oven temperature to 375° F.

2. Bring a saucepan of salted water to a boil. Add the potato slices and cook until just tender, 4–5 minutes. Drain well and set aside.

3. Heat the olive oil in a skillet and add the leeks, garlic, and thyme. Cook gently until softened, but not browned, 10 minutes. Remove from the heat and let cool slightly.

4. To assemble the tart, spread the leek mixture over the pastry base. Lay the potato slices on top. Arrange the goat cheese slices on top of the potatoes. Whisk the egg yolks and cream together with some seasoning until smooth, then pour into the pastry case. Scatter with pine nuts and bake until set and golden, 25–30 minutes. Let cool 15 minutes before serving.

Crumble topped blueberry pie with cinnamon pastry

For the pastry • 1 ½ cups all-purpose flour • pinch salt • 1 tsp. ground cinnamon • ½ cup butter, diced • 3–4 tbsp. cold water
For the filling • 1 ½ lbs. blueberries • ⅓ cup sugar
For the crumble topping • generous 1 ¼ cups all-purpose flour • pinch salt • ½ cup butter, diced • ⅓ cup brown sugar • ⅓ cup flaked almonds

SERVES 6–8

1. Prepare the pastry following steps 1–4 in the basic shortcrust pastry method (see pages 106–7), adding the cinnamon to the flour and salt and mixing well. Roll the pastry into a rough circle at least 2 inches larger than a 2-inch deep, loose-bottomed 9-inch fluted pastry ring. Gently roll the pastry onto the rolling pin, then unroll it over the ring to cover. Carefully press the pastry into the edges. Prick the base all over with a fork. Refrigerate for 20 minutes.

2. Preheat the oven to 400° F. Line the pastry case with foil or waxed paper and fill with baking beans. Transfer to the oven and bake for 12 minutes. Remove the baking beans and foil and cook for a further 10 minutes until golden. Remove from the oven and set aside to cool.

3. Mix the blueberries and sugar. Set aside.

4. For the crumble topping, put the flour and salt into a large bowl. Add the butter and rub into the flour until coarsely combined, with largish lumps of butter still showing. Stir in the sugar. Spoon the blueberries into the pastry case and top evenly with the crumb mixture. Sprinkle over the flaked almonds.

5. Transfer to the oven and bake until golden and bubbling, 20–25 minutes. Let cool and serve warm or cold with whipped cream.

Spiced palmiers with apples and raisins

For the palmiers • **1 quantity puff pastry (see page 116)** • **4 tbsp. sugar** • **2 tbsp. confectioners' sugar** • **1 tsp. ground cinnamon** • **½ tsp. ground ginger** • **½ tsp. grated nutmeg** • **generous ½ cup heavy cream, lightly whipped, to serve**
For the apple and raisin compote • **1 lb. tart apples, roughly chopped** • **4 tbsp. sugar** • **1 tbsp. raisins** • **1 tbsp. dried cherries or cranberries** • **2 tsp. grated orange peel**

MAKES about 36 cookies

These little cookies are delightfully tasty served with a tangy apple compote and fresh cream.

1. Prepare the basic puff pastry method (see pages 114–5). Roll the pastry thinly and trim to a 10- x 16-inch rectangle. Cut in two to make two smaller rectangles. Sift the sugar, confectioners' sugar, cinnamon, ginger, and nutmeg together. Dust both sides of both pastry sheets with about a quarter of the spiced sugar.

2. Working one rectangle at a time, lay the pastry in front of you with one long edge nearest you. Fold the pastry in half, away from you, then unfold to give a crease down the middle. Fold the edge of the pastry nearest you halfway to the crease and repeat with the edge of the pastry furthest from you. Dust liberally with more of the spiced sugar.

3. Repeat the fold so that the edge nearest you meets the edge furthest from you in the middle where you creased the pastry originally. Dust again with sugar. Reserve any sugar that you have leftover for later.

4. Finally, fold again down the crease to give a long thin rectangle. This will give you six layers in all. Repeat with the second rectangle. Wrap each in plastic wrap and put into the freezer to rest, 1 hour.

5. Preheat the oven to 350° F. Remove the pastry from the freezer and dust with any remaining spiced sugar. Using a sharp knife, cut each crosswise into eighteen slices. Lay slices well spaced apart on a baking sheet and transfer to the oven. Bake 10 minutes, then turn and bake until golden, 5–10 minutes. Cool on a wire rack.

6. Meanwhile, put all the apple compote ingredients into a saucepan. Cover and cook over a gentle heat until the apple is soft, about 15 minutes. Stir well and set aside to cool.

7. To serve, put the apple compote into a serving bowl, put the whipped cream into a second bowl, and arrange the cookies on a dish.

Coffee and walnut pie

generous 1 cup all-purpose flour • pinch salt • ⅓ cup butter, diced • 2–3 tbsp. cold water • ¾ cup maple syrup • 1 tbsp. instant coffee granules • 1 tbsp. boiling water • 2 tbsp. butter, softened • ⅔ cup golden brown sugar • 3 eggs, beaten • 1 tsp. vanilla extract • ⅔ cup walnut halves • whipped cream or ice cream to serve

SERVES 4–6

If you like pecan pie, you'll love this coffee-maple-walnut alternative.

1. Make the pastry following steps 1-6 in the basic shortcrust pastry method (pages 106–7). Preheat the oven to 400° F. Line the pastry case with foil or waxed paper and fill with baking beans. Transfer to the oven and bake for 12 minutes. Remove the baking beans and foil and cook for a further 10 minutes until golden. Remove from the oven and leave to cool. Reduce the oven temperature to 350° F.

2. Put the maple syrup into a saucepan and heat until almost boiling. Mix the coffee granules with the boiling water, stirring until they have completely dissolved. Stir this mixture into the maple syrup. Leave until just warm.

3. Mix the butter with the sugar until combined, then gradually beat in the eggs. Add the cooled maple syrup mixture along with the vanilla extract and stir well.

4. Arrange the walnut halves in the bottom of the pastry case, then carefully pour in the filling. Transfer to the oven and bake until browned and firm, 30–35 minutes. Let cool about 10 minutes. Serve with cream or ice cream.

Old-fashioned peach and raspberry pies

For the pastry • **1 ¾ cups all-purpose flour** • **pinch salt** • **½ cup butter, diced** • **3–4 tbsp. cold water**
For the filling • **4 large ripe peaches, pitted and roughly chopped** • **1 cup raspberries** • **⅓ cup sugar, plus extra for sprinkling** • **juice ½ lemon** • **1 tbsp. milk** • **sour cream, to serve**

SERVES 4

1. Make the pastry following steps 1–3 in the basic shortcrust pastry method (see pages 106–7).

2. Mix together the peaches, raspberries, sugar, and lemon juice and set aside.

3. Preheat the oven to 400° F. Divide the pastry into four equal portions. Working with one portion at a time, divide into one-third and two-thirds. Roll out the larger piece to fit a 4-inch individual round pie pan. Add a quarter of the peach mixture. Wet the edges of the pastry and roll out the smaller portion of pastry. Use to top the pie, trimming off the excess and crimping the edges to seal. Snip a cross or hole in the top of the pie to allow steam to escape.

4. Brush the pastry with a little milk and sprinkle with sugar. Repeat to make four pies. Transfer the pies to the oven and bake until the pastry is golden, about 20–25 minutes.

5. Let cool about 10 minutes, then carefully turn the pies out of their pans. Serve with sour cream.

Linzertorte with a lattice top

1½ cups all-purpose flour • pinch salt • ⅓ cup ground almonds • ½ cup + 2 tbsp. unsalted butter, diced • 4 tbsp. golden brown sugar • 2 eggs, separated • 3–4 tsp. cold water • 1 lb. fresh raspberries • ½ cup sugar • 2 tsp. cornstarch mixed with 2 tsp. cold water • 1 tbsp. fresh lemon juice • confectioners' sugar, to decorate • heavy cream, to serve

SERVES 8

1. For the pastry, mix the flour, salt and almonds. Add the butter and rub in until the mixture resembles fine bread crumbs. Stir in the golden brown sugar. Mix the egg yolks with the cold water. Add to the pastry and bring the dough together. Knead briefly until smooth. Wrap in plastic wrap and chill 30 minutes.

2. Put the raspberries and sugar into a saucepan over a low heat. Bring to a boil, stir in the cornstarch mixture and cook 2 minutes. Remove from the heat, stir in the lemon juice and leave until cold.

3. Preheat the oven to 400° F. Put a heavy baking sheet on the center shelf to preheat with the oven. Roll out about two-thirds of the pastry and use to line a loose-bottomed 8-inch deep fluted pastry ring, following steps 4, 5, and 6 in the basic shortcrust pastry method (see pages 106–7). Remove trimmings and reroll with the remaining pastry. Cut into ten long strips, each ¾-inch wide using a zigzag cutter.

4. Spoon the raspberry mixture into the pastry case. Dampen the edges of the pastry using the egg white, then lay the pastry strips over the top of the filling to make a lattice pattern. Lightly press the edges of the pastry together, and trim off excess pastry.

5. Put the tart on the preheated baking sheet and bake, 20–25 minutes until the pastry is golden. Let cool 5 minutes. Remove from the ring and leave an additional 10–15 minutes. Dust with confectioners' sugar. Serve warm cut into wedges with cream.

Freeform strawberry rhubarb pie

For the pastry • **generous 1 cup all-purpose flour** • **pinch salt** • **⅓ cup butter, diced** • **½ cup ground almonds** • **¼ cup sugar** • **3–4 tbsp. cold water**
For the filling • **2¾ cups rhubarb, cut into chunks** • **⅓-½ cup sugar, to taste** • **1 vanilla bean** • **2 strips lemon zest** • **2 tsp. cornstarch or ground arrowroot** • **1 cup strawberries, hulled and halved if large** • **2 tsp. coarse sugar**   **SERVES 4–6**

1. Make the pastry following steps 1–3 in the basic shortcrust pastry method (see pages 106–7), adding the ground almonds and sugar to the rubbed in mixture. You may need a little extra water to bind this pastry.

2. Put the rhubarb, ⅓ cup of the sugar, vanilla bean, and lemon zest into a saucepan over a gentle heat. Cook, stirring often, until the rhubarb is tender and quite juicy but still holding its shape, about 8–10 minutes. Taste for sweetness and add the remaining sugar if necessary.

3. Mix the cornstarch with a little water until smooth. Stir into the rhubarb, return the mixture to a gentle simmer. Cook until thickened, about 1–2 minutes.

4. Remove from the heat and stir in the strawberries and set aside until cold. Remove the vanilla bean and lemon zest.

5. Preheat the oven to 400° F. Roll out the pastry to a large circle about 15 inches in diameter. Transfer to a large, nonstick baking sheet. Spoon the cold strawberry-rhubarb mixture into the middle of the pastry and gather the pastry around the filling, leaving an open top. Brush the pastry with a little cold water and sprinkle with the coarse sugar.

6. Transfer the baking sheet to the center of the oven and bake, about 20-25 minutes. When cold, serve cut into wedges.

Lemon chiffon pie

For the pastry • generous 1 cup all-purpose flour • pinch salt • ⅓ cup butter, diced • ¼ cup sugar • 2 tsp. grated lemon peel • 2 tbsp. cold water • 1 egg yolk
For the filling • ¾ cup sugar • 3 eggs and 2 egg whites • 3 large lemons, grated zest and juice • ⅓ cup butter

SERVES 6–8

1. For the pastry, follow step 1 in the basic shortcrust pastry method (see pages 106–7). Stir the sugar and lemon peel into the rubbed in mixture. Mix together the cold water and egg yolk and add to the dough. Bring the dough together, adding a little more water if necessary. Follow steps 3–6 in the basic shortcrust pastry method.

2. Reduce the oven temperature to 300° F.

3. For the filling, in a large heatproof bowl, whisk together ⅓ cup of the sugar, the whole eggs, the lemon zest and juice, and butter. Put the bowl over a pan of simmering water and continue whisking until thick, about 15 minutes. Remove the bowl from the heat and put the base of the bowl into cold water—either in the sink or in a larger bowl. Continue whisking until the mixture has cooled.

4. Beat the egg whites until stiff then gradually beat in the remaining sugar until thick and shiny. Fold one large spoonful of this mixture into the lemon mixture to slacken it, then fold in the remaining egg whites. Pour into the pastry case.

5. Bake in the center of the oven until just set, 25–30 minutes. Cool on a wire rack before serving.

Upside-down pear tart with cardamom

½ cup sugar • 3–4 tbsp. cold water • about 10 green cardamom pods • 4–6 ripe but firm pears, depending on size, cored and quartered lengthwise • ¼ cup unsalted butter, diced • ½ quantity puff pastry (see page 116), prepared to the end of step 6 (see pages 114–15) • sour cream to serve

SERVES 4–6

This is really a Tarte Tatin made with pears. Cardamom is a surprisingly effective flavor with pears.

1. Put the sugar and water into a 10-inch ovenproof skillet. Stir over a low heat until the sugar has dissolved completely. Increase the heat and bring the mixture to a rapid simmer.

2. Remove seeds from cardamom and finely crush. As soon as the sugar begins to color, sprinkle over the cardamom. Do not stir. Carefully add the pear quarters in concentric circles. The sugar will slow down, but you must watch it now as you want it to color evenly. Tilt and turn the pan often until the sugar bubbling up between the pears is deep brown and smells nutty. Immediately remove from the heat and add butter wherever there are spaces between the fruit. Let cool about 20 minutes.

3. Preheat the oven to 400° F. Roll out the prepared pastry thinly then cut a circle about 1 inch larger than the diameter of the skillet. Carefully put the pastry over the pears, tucking it down the sides of the pan to enclose the fruit.

4. Transfer the skillet to the oven and bake until the pastry is risen and golden, 25 minutes.

5. Remove from the oven and leave to stand about 10 minutes before carefully turning out onto a serving plate. Serve warm, cut into wedges, with sour cream.

Banana toffee cheesecake

For the pastry • **1 ¼ cups all-purpose flour** • **pinch salt** • **½ cup butter, diced** • **¼ cup sugar** •
3–4 tbsp. cold water
For the filling • **1 cup unsweetened chocolate, broken into pieces, plus extra for decoration** •
14-oz can sweetened condensed milk • **1 cup mascarpone cheese** • **½ cup heavy cream,**
lightly whipped • **3 large ripe but firm bananas** • **½ lemon, juice only**   **SERVES 10–12**

1. For the pastry, follow steps 1, 2 and 3 in the basic shortcrust pastry
method (see pages 106–7), stirring the sugar into the rubbed in mixture.

2. Follow step 4 of the basic shortcrust pastry method, rolling the pastry
into a large circle about 2 inches larger than a 9-inch plain pastry ring set
on a baking tray. Ease the pastry into the ring following steps 5 and 6 of
the basic shortcrust pastry method. Preheat the oven to 400° F. Line the
pastry case with foil or waxed paper and fill with baking beans. Transfer to
the oven and bake for 12 minutes. Remove the baking beans and foil and
cook for a further 10-12 minutes until golden. Remove from the oven and
let cool. Carefully brush off any crumbs from inside the pastry case.

3. Melt the chocolate in a bowl set over a pan of simmering water.
Using a pastry brush, paint the chocolate onto the pastry case to cover
completely. Refrigerate until set.

4. Meanwhile, for the toffee pour the can of sweetened condensed milk
into the top of a double boiler; place over boiling water. Over a low heat,
simmer 1 to 1½ hours or until thick and caramel colored. Beat until
smooth. Remove the double boiler from the heat and allow to cool.

5. To assemble the cheesecake, thickly slice the bananas and drizzle with
the lemon juice. Set aside. Beat the mascarpone cheese until softened
then stir in the cream. Carefully fold the cream and toffee mixtures together
but don't overmix—leave them marbled. Fold in the bananas, then spoon
the mixture into the pastry case. Grate remaining chocolate over the top.

Tarte fine aux pommes

½ quantity puff pastry (see pages 116), prepared to the end of step 6 (see pages 114–15) • 2 dessert apples • 1½ tbsp confectioners' sugar • 2 tbsp. apricot jelly • cream, to serve

SERVES 4

1. Prepare the puff pastry following the basic method on pages 114–15. Roll the pasty out thinly and cut out a 9-inch circle. Transfer to a lightly greased baking sheet.

2. Preheat the oven to 375° F. Halve the apples and thinly slice lengthwise. Lay on the pastry in concentric circles, overlapping slightly and leaving a ½-inch margin around the edge. Dust generously with the confectioners' sugar.

3. Transfer the baking sheet to the oven and bake until the pastry is risen and golden and the apples are tender and golden at the edges, 20–25 minutes.

4. Gently heat the apricot jelly in a small saucepan then press through a sieve to remove any large pieces. While the jelly and tart are both hot, brush the jelly generously over the apple slices to glaze. Leave to cool slightly and serve warm with cold cream.

index

suppliers

Bed, Bath & Beyond
800-GO-BEYOND
www.bedbathandbeyond.com

Chef's
P.O. Box 620048
Dallas, TX 75262
800-884-CHEF
www.chefscatalog.com

Cooking.com
2850 Ocean Park Blvd. Ste. 310
Santa Monica, CA 90405
800-663-8810
www.cooking.com

Crate & Barrel
800-967-6696
www.crateandbarrel.com

Dean & Deluca
560 Brodway
New York, NY 10012
877-826-9246
www.deandeluca.com

House 2 Home
3345 Michelson Drive
Irvine, CA 92612
1-877-980-7467
www.house2home.com

IKEA
Plymouth Meeting Mall
498 W. Germantown Pike
Plymouth Meeting, PA 19462
610-834-1520
www.ikea.com

Kitchen Etc.
32 Industrial Drive
Exeter, NH 03833
800-232-4070
www.kitchenetc.com

OurHouse.com
1880 Oak Ave.
Evanston, IL 60201
877-202-2768

Peppercorn
1235 Pearl Street
Boulder, CO 80302
800-447-6905
www.peppercorn.com

Pier 1 Imports
800-245-4595
www.pier1.com

Restoration Hardware
15 Koch Rd. Ste. J
Corte Madera, CA 94925
877-747-4671
www.restorationhardware.com

Target
888-304-4000
www.target.com

Williams-Sonoma
3250 Van Ness Ave.
San Francisco, CA 94109
877-812-6235
www.williams-sonoma.com